Private Lives

Private Lives

studies of birds and other animals from
the BBC tv wildlife series *Look* and
Private Lives
edited by Jeffery Boswall

British Broadcasting Corporation

To Hans Sielmann
whose woodpecker film was the inspiration

*The aim of science should certainly be to remove the
mystery from natural phenomena, but not to take away
wonder, or that quality of nature which allows for the
development and play of aesthetic appreciation.* FRANK FRASER DARLING

Published by the British Broadcasting Corporation,
35 Marylebone High Street, London, W1M 4AA

First published 1970
© British Broadcasting Corporation and contributors 1970
SBN 563 08591 6

Photoset by BAS Printers Limited,
Wallop, Hampshire
Printed in England by Sir Joseph Causton and Sons Ltd,
33–39 Savile Row, London W1

Contents

Acknowledgement is due to the following for permission to reproduce illustrations on the following pages:

Amateur Gardening 134, 135, 140, 141
Eric Ashby 154, 156
Jane Burton/Bruce Coleman Ltd   34, facing 48 top and bottom, facing 49, 130, 131
R. Balharry 80, facing 80 bottom, facing 81
S. Bisserôt/Bruce Coleman Ltd   127
J. Morton Boyd facing 8 top
S. Beaufoy 105 top and bottom, 106, 107, 108, 109, 110
J. Belling 80
W. N. Charles 90, 91, 92, 93, 98, 99, 100 bottom
Peter Condall/Harold Dellman 119
J. T. Darby 24, 27, 28
Rose Eastman facing 16 top, 50, 51, 52, 62, facing 64 top and bottom, facing
    65 top and bottom, facing 97 bottom, facing 104 top, facing 144 top
J. D. Gibson facing 112, facing 113 bottom, 119, 120, 121, facing 128 bottom
Hilmar Hansen facing 32 middle, 35
Peter Hinchliffe/Bruce Coleman Ltd 12
John Hooper 66, 67, 68, 69, 70, 71 top and bottom, facing 72, 72, 76, 77
Eric Hosking 9 top, 10, 13, 15, 38, 116, 117, 118, facing 104 bottom, 143, 144
    (Niall Rankin)
Geoffrey Kinns 43 top and bottom, 47, 125, 128, 129, facing 129, facing 152
Frank Lane (Lynwood M. Chace) 23, (Wilford L. Miller) 42,
    (H. Hoflinger) facing 96, (Ronald Thompson) 99, 100
Marconi Company Ltd 145, 146
John Markham 41
Tanu M. Mitchev 53
P. Morris 126, 129, 132 top and bottom
Mougin 18, 19, 21, 22, 26
P. K. Murton/Bruce Coleman Ltd facing 16 bottom
Harold Oldroyd/Natural Science Photos facing 153 top
C. E. Palmar 136
H. Pasmore facing 148, 148, 153 bottom
L. Perkins/Natural Science Photos facing 33 top
Ivan Polinin 30
J. Prevost 20, 21, 23, 25
Rentokil Laboratories Ltd 142
T. Soper 79
B. Stonehouse facing 17
Sunday Telegraph 9 bottom
P. O. Swanberg 54 top and bottom, 55 top and bottom, 61
Gerald Thompson 103 top and bottom, 104, facing 105, 111
W. L. N. Tickell facing 113 top, 121, facing 128 top
Barrie Thomas/Bruce Coleman Ltd facing 73
R. Tweddle 81, 85, 86, 87
Stephanie Tyler 149, 151, 155
Ilkka Virkkunen 48, facing 97 top, facing 144 bottom, facing 145 top and bottom
Gene Wolfsheimer 31, facing 32 top and bottom, facing 33 bottom
Bruce R. Young 139
The drawings on pages 11, 31, 33, 67, 94, 95, 97, 114, 115 (from Peter Shepheard's original drawing 'The Wandering Albatross' by William Jameson) and 123 are by Maurice Wilson. The drawing on page 76 is by Joanna C. Webb. The remaining diagrams and drawings are by Roger Durban. The maps on pages 73 and 74 were re-drawn by permission of The Zoological Society of London, and those on pages 82 and 84 by permission of the Controller of H.M. Stationery Office.

Introduction *Sir Julian Huxley, F.R.S.*

In 1935 I was involved in the making of a film that was to have the title 'The Private Life of the Gannets'. With the aid of Ronald Lockley, the Pembrokeshire ornithologist, who had first shown me this wonderful gannetry, I directed the film and spoke the commentary, while the brilliant cameraman was Osmond Borrodaile, from London Films, Sir Alexander Korda's company, which produced the film. Sir Alexander was, I think, excited by a subject so new to him. He had just produced the epic 'Private Life of Henry VIII' and this certainly had something to do with the title chosen for the bird film. Be that as it may, our film was probably the first to be made in Britain to be devoted entirely to a single species of wild creature. In 1937 the film won a Hollywood 'Oscar' – an award of the American Academy of Motion Picture Arts and Sciences – as the best 'one-reel short' of the year.

In the thirty-odd years that have elapsed since then more films have been made depicting the life-cycles of individual species. One that comes at once to mind is the famous woodpecker film of Hans Sielmann's which I saw at the International Ornithological Congress at Basle in 1954. Although not devoted to a single species – it wisely dealt with the Great Spotted and Green Woodpeckers as well as the Black – it was a classic example of intimate movie presentation of the way wild creatures live.

The film was introduced to British television viewers by Peter Scott, whose long-running series *Look* included more films about single species. Thus, Eric Ashby, the 'silent watcher' of the New Forest, relentlessly and patiently pursued wild foxes with his movie camera, and in the icy Antarctic the French naturalist Jean Prevost filmed the strange home life of the Emperor Penguin.

But the *Look* film I remember best is Ron and Rosemary Eastman's 'Private Life of the Kingfisher' which I saw in colour at the London Zoo. I was captivated by the close-up shots of our most brilliantly plumaged bird, and the detailed coverage of the species' habits and life-cycle. The success of that film, I am told, gave rise to this new series of wildlife television films under the general title *Private Lives*, and hence to this book.

I was fortunate enough to be given a personal advance screening of all but one of the new series at the BBC's little theatre in Maida Vale. 'The Private Life of the Starling' took my mind back to the first bird-watching I ever did. It was in the attic of our house at

Godalming in Surrey where I watched parent starlings feeding their brood.

Life histories are always interesting and few among fish can show greater biological interest and variety than the behaviour of the Siamese Fighter, *Betta splendens*. Ron Eastman filmed both of these, and also 'The Private Life of the Robin'. David Lack (our great expert on robins) was scientific adviser for this remarkable cine-study and tells me that the film depicts certain aspects of bird behaviour more clearly than he was able to observe them in nature. Praise indeed!

'The Private Life of the Large White Butterfly' and its handsomer relatives like the Brimstone and the Orange Tip is a wonderfully clear photographic record. Never have I seen such marvellous close-up photography as that achieved here by Gerald Thompson at Oxford.

Most viewers will be familiar with the 'cabbage' white; few will have ever seen a Wandering Albatross. Its domestic affairs, including its fantastic mutual courtship displays, are brought splendidly to the screen by Lancelot Tickell who lived among these giant wanderers in a breeding colony on the sub-Antarctic island of South Georgia.

The shooting of the sixth 'Private Life', that of the Great Crested Grebe, is still in progress as this book goes to press. A favourite of mine, I gave the first scientific description and interpretation of the grebe's strange and lovely 'courtship' as long ago as 1914. It has the most fantastic sexual display of any British bird. I much look forward to seeing the film on my colour set.

I am told that *Private Lives* is the first wildlife series produced in colour for BBC 1 by the BBC Natural History Unit. I congratulate the Unit and wish the series and the accompanying book every possible success. I hope that there will be more *Private Lives* to follow. Perhaps my own 'Private Life of the Gannets' could be remade in colour? I hope so.

September 1969   Julian Huxley

The Robin   *David Lack*

Recently a ballot was taken for the bird which would provide the most suitable emblem for the British section of an international body concerned with bird preservation. No one was surprised when the robin *(Erithacus rubecula)* came clear ahead of all possible rivals. It is best known for two reasons, first its tameness, and secondly its habit of nesting in strange places. Its tameness presents a fascinating biological problem, but its nesting sites are a mere curiosity, because the places where a robin sometimes nests are strange only to us. In its native woods the bird builds in a shallow hole or covered niche in dense cover, but in tidying our gardens we tend to remove such hidden niches, so it seeks the substitutes which we leave about. To us it is curious to find its nest in an old teapot in a ditch, in the pocket of a jacket hung in a shed, in the lectern of a church or in the panel of a parked aircraft, but to the robin these may not look appreciably different from its natural holes.

Feeding behaviour and tameness

Its tameness is another matter, for no other British bird behaves in this way towards men. As soon as we start digging in the garden the local robin is there to watch, and to drop down to pick up the worms or larvae which we turn up. This behaviour is found even in the speckled young in August, which could not by then have learned that a gardener might provide them with food, so the behaviour is at least partly inherited. This in turn must mean that the ability finds, or found formerly, a place in the natural life of the bird. The robin hunts either by sitting on a perch above the ground and dropping down to pick up small insects on the surface, or by hopping about the ground looking for them. But the creatures that live in the soil and the leaf-litter are often just below the surface and, especially in very cold weather, they move down, and then the robin cannot break the frozen surface to get at them. At these times, in particular, it follows any animal that may break up the soil, not only a man with a spade, but large birds such as the pheasant, which scratch up the soil with their strong toes, and even small mammals like the mole, which burrow just below the surface. A robin has been seen to snatch a worm almost from the mouth of a mole. Perhaps it once followed wild boars in a similar way, as these regularly root in the soil. Almost all the other insect-eating

A discarded can (above) or even an umpire's coat pocket may seem unusual to us as a nest-site, but to a robin they may not look appreciably different from natural holes

9

The robin will follow any animal that may break up the soil, including man

birds of northern Europe migrate south for the winter, but the robin is able to remain because it can utilise the habits of other animals in this way.

From flying down to pick up larvae disturbed by the spade, it is but a short step for the robin to take food from the hand, and it is much more easily tamed to do so than any other British bird. If encouraged, it will even enter the house, though, as the great naturalist Gilbert White remarked, 'it spoils the furniture.' It enters houses particularly in Germany, where the winters are cold, and the bird not only gains shelter and warmth for the night, but can pick up any insects in the house, which in former times included bed bugs. A German correspondent suggested to me that this habit could have originated from the bird seeking out, in primeval times, the caves of wild bears, which would likewise have provided it with shelter and some food. So in accepting the tame robin, man is almost certainly inheriting a natural habit evolved in relation to wild animals in the past. How long robins have sought out man in this way is not known, but we have no reason to suppose that the first recorded taming of a robin, by St Serf in the sixth century A.D., was by any means the first. Our cave-dwelling ancestors several millenniums earlier might have been hosts to the bird.

Defending a territory

The robin is famous for one more reason, that it fights for and maintains a territory, from which all other adult robins are driven except its own mate. Indeed this habit provides the first mention of the robin in literature. 'One bush does not shelter two robins' was a proverb at least by the third century B.C. Many other songbirds maintain a territory when breeding, though perhaps less intensively than the robin, but the latter is exceptional in maintaining its territory almost throughout the year. It may stop defending it while it moults in late summer, but even during this depressing time it continues to live in it. It proclaims its ownership by singing from the trees, and the birds in adjoining territories sing back. At intervals they move towards each other, first one singing and then the other, until they reach their common boundary, where they sing more agitatedly for a short time, perhaps with some display, but the boundary is well known from previous encounters and they soon retire again.

It is easy to show that a robin has a territory, for if one walks after it, it moves away until it reaches the boundary, when it rises higher in the trees and eventually flies back over one's head. Except when claiming a new or enlarged territory, a robin never sings outside its own domain. But though so keen in preserving its ground, it trespasses freely for food, keeping as hidden as possible, and if the owner of the land in question sees it and gives chase, it puts up no resistance and quickly returns to its own ground. The owner hardly ever needs to strike an intruder to make it retire. If its song alone does not suffice, it flies down to the trespasser, stops a few feet away and sways its body from side to side, stretching out the red breast to make it as conspicuous as possible and fluffing out its other feathers too, all the while warbling intensely. This threat display is almost always effective and, as the intruder departs, the owner chases it over the boundary. The display of the red breast can readily be watched in one's garden if the boundary between two territories happens to be situated there, as one can often tempt one of the birds to trespass by putting out food near the boundary.

Much more serious and prolonged encounters occur when a newcomer robin seeks to stake out a territory by displacing the owner-occupier. This elicits the finest song of the whole year as each cock answers the other. At intervals they break off and display their red breasts, and as the newcomer does not depart, they then grapple with each other, and may even fall to the ground pecking hard at each other's faces. The newcomer sometimes gives up at this stage, but if it is persistent, the pecking grows more serious, many feathers are lost and blood is drawn. Rarely, one robin kills another, usually by pecking through the base of its skull, but it happens so rarely that I never saw it in four years of intensive watching, though there are published records of it by reliable observers. The point is important for understanding the significance of the threat display. As already stressed, when the owner of the territory finds another robin there, it first sings, and if this does not make it leave, it displays vigorously. The same happens with many other kinds of birds, and also with other kinds of animals. Some people have argued that it should therefore be possible for man to reduce his aggressive behaviour to a threat display, thus eliminating war. But this rests on a mistaken interpretation of what happens in nature. If neither song nor postures make the intruder go, the owning robin grapples with it and strikes it, and this continues until one of them gives up, by which time it may be seriously hurt or, in rare cases, killed. Threat display has been evolved because, if it suffices, it gives both combatants the best chance of survival, the victor obviously, but the loser also if it is going to lose anyway and can retreat before it is hurt, for then it has the chance of finding a territory elsewhere. But it would not be advantageous for the potential loser to retreat unless it would otherwise be badly hurt or killed, for there may well be no other suitable ground vacant. Hence the threat must potentially be capable of enforcement. Probably the most serious fights occur when both owner and newcomer have a strong aggressive drive, and when, in addition, they remain unaware which of them is likely to be the loser. Since if threat fails force is used, there is here no moral lesson for man.

Aggressive posture of the robin. According to
the relative height of the intruder the defending robin exposes
the maximum area of his red breast towards him.

Robin attacking stuffed 'intruder' in its territory

Experiment with a stuffed robin

Perhaps the easiest way to see how a robin fights is to put out a stuffed one. Once the owner of the territory notices it, it descends and displays its red breast to it. If the only available perch is above the stuffed intruder, the robin stretches out its breast horizontally and downwards; while if it is below, it points its beak skyward or even backwards. In both attitudes, the greatest possible area of red is directed at the intruder. A stuffed bird cannot, of course, retreat, and after excited postures, the owner then attacks. A live intruder would at this point face it and grapple with its feet, but since the stuffed bird does not do this, the owner then moves behind it to strike at the base of its skull. If it had been alive, the blows here would have killed it. As it is, I have on several occasions had the head of a stuffed robin struck off. As the owner then continued its attacks, it led me to experiment on just how much of a specimen was needed to evoke attack. I found that to elicit threat display, only the red breast was needed, and that it evoked much more display than did a whole stuffed robin on which I had painted the red breast brown. The red breast alone was not struck by the owning robin, whereas the all-brown robin, though not postured at, was sometimes struck. Experiments such as this show how different from ours must be the world that a robin sees.

Territorial defence occupies almost all the daylight hours of a robin that are not spent in feeding or breeding. What, then, is the purpose of the territory? This remains in great dispute. The bird breeds in its territory, and does not breed if it has not got one, and the same applies to many other songbirds, but why they need breeding territories is not clear, for many other species dispense with them. Probably the territory helps the bird to get a mate, and to keep it once obtained. As a minister in the Church of Scotland who was interested in this subject remarked: 'If I go to Edinburgh with my wife and wish to find her again, I need either to have a fixed address or to follow her about the whole time.' The same, as he pointed out, holds with wild birds. In those which pair in flocks the male and female keep constantly together, which must sometimes hamper them, whereas in territorial species the cock has a fixed address, where the hen first finds him and to which he and she always return.

Pairing up and nesting

Pair-formation takes place in England from late December onward, long before the traditional St Valentine's Day. The cock is here faced with a problem because, until that moment, he has driven every other robin from his territory. But if he continued to do so, he would never get a mate! As it is, when an unmated hen first comes along, the cock sings and displays as if in a fight, and she replies similarly, so that I several times misinterpreted the first stage of pair-formation as a fight and knew that the second bird was a hen only when they had been colour-ringed for individual recognition. Sometimes such sparring lasts as long as two days, but the birds get used to each other, and thereafter the hen is accepted in the territory. Even after that, however, feathers tend to bristle if she comes too close to him.

There is then a long quiescent period, lasting two and sometimes three months, after which the hen starts to bring material to form a nest. Around this time the cock also starts feeding the hen with caterpillars or worms, and he continues to do so throughout egg-

*A newly fledged robin
has protectively speckled plumage,
making it less conspicuous to predators*

laying and incubation. I used to think this was a purely symbolic gesture, like a man giving his fiancée chocolates, but now realise that the food brought may itself be important. The eggs are laid at the end of winter, when food is only just beginning to be plentiful, and if the cock feeds the hen, she may be able to lay earlier. Fitting this view, when Ronald and Rosemary Eastman were making their film *The Private Life of the Robin*, the tamed robins provided with mealworms during the winter bred a month earlier than usual. The food brought by the cock may be at least as valuable during incubation, since only the hen sits on the eggs, so she has to come off periodically to feed, and if the cock brings her food in this time, she can return quickly to the eggs.

After the eggs hatch, both parents spend almost the whole day feeding the chicks. In the wild, where they nest chiefly in oak woods, they bring especially the green caterpillars which, during the day, lie under oak leaves. Caterpillars are not nearly so plentiful in gardens, and here the birds bring a more varied diet. Another idea about the robin's territory is that it helps the parents to conserve a supply of food near their nest, but this is not certain, as other woodland birds bring the same kinds of caterpillars to their young, and the robin does not exclude these other species from its territory. After the young of the first brood leave the nest, the cock continues to feed them for two or three weeks, while the hen starts a second brood, which the cock is ready to help in feeding by the time that the young hatch.

The parents not only feed their young but protect them, mainly by giving alarm calls, at which the nestlings crouch low in the nest and the fledglings keep motionless in cover, helped by their

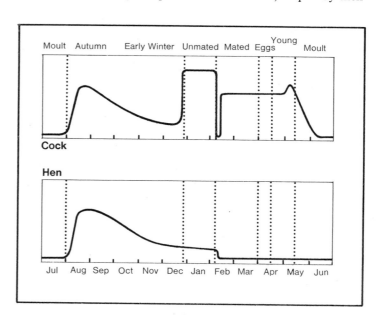

Seasonal variation in song output of cock and hen robins

*The robin lays up a store
of subcutaneous fat to increase
its chances of winter survival*

concealing colouring. If a mammal like a cat approaches, the adult robin bobs up and down on a twig, safely out of range, giving a rattled *tic-tic-tick*. But if it sees a hawk, it sits motionless and utters a high-pitched long-drawn *see-eep*, hard to locate. Such ventriloquial 'hawk-alarm' notes are also found in various other songbirds, and they serve to warn the young without showing the hawk where the adult is.

Autumn and winter

In July, when breeding is finished, the parent robins moult, and near the end of this time the young lose their spotted plumage and acquire red breasts. Then virtually all the adult cocks and some of the hens and young stake out individual territories, while the other hens and young migrate south for the winter, where they also stake out individual territories. The hen robin, like the cock, defends her territory by song and by threatening with her red breast. If only the resident cocks had defended territories in autumn, one might have argued that they do so merely to ensure possession of a territory for breeding in the following spring. But both the resident hens and the migrants of both sexes leave their winter territories in spring, so they have no function in relation to breeding.

One probable advantage of a winter territory lies in the robin's way of hunting. It often sits quietly on a perch and pounces on small insects moving on the ground below. This way of hunting might be disturbed if another robin perched close to it, and maintenance of a territory prevents this. Other birds which hunt in the same way, such as shrikes and desert wheatears, are, with the robin, among the few birds which defend individual territories in winter. It is doubtful, however, whether this provides a sufficient explanation, and some workers suggest that each robin defends a sufficient area to supply it with food for the winter. This has not been checked, but it would be hard to measure the food supply of a robin. Perhaps pointing against this is the frequency with which robins trespass for food. They respect each other's territories for pairing and nesting, but not for food.

It is surprising that the explanation should still be doubtful for such a well-known fact of natural history as the robin's territory. Personally, I am further disappointed that no one has studied the robin since my own observations were completed thirty years ago. These observations must have been incomplete, and it would be surprising if they did not also need correcting, yet no one has yet checked them, though most of my later research has been re-examined by others. Part of the explanation may be that the robin is most easily studied by someone resident in the British Isles, for only here is it so tame, and only here can it readily be watched in English gardens or open countryside. In most of the rest of its range it lives in forests, and to study a wild bird in a forest is a much harder proposition. I therefore hope that the magnificent film made by the Eastmans will not only be enjoyed by many, but that it will be studied in detail by some, who will then be stimulated to discover new things about this redoubtable little bird.

The cock feeds the hen during egg-laying and incubation

Robin delivering caterpillar to young in natural nesting site

Emperors at Cape Royale

The Emperor Penguin *Bernard Stonehouse*

Emperor penguins (*Aptenodytes forsteri*) are at home on the cold coast of the Antarctic continent. Hatched and reared on floating sea ice, they spend most of their life within sight of ice – the pack ice of Antarctic waters, or the age-old glacier ice of the polar continent. Emperors are the largest penguins and the most colourful. Their yellow shirts, golden ear patches and purple-sheathed bills make a welcome splash of warmth among the white, green and blue of Antarctica's palette. One emperor on its own is spectacular; a colony of thousands, at home in a setting of ice cliffs, mountains and deep blue skies, is a truly magnificent sight.

Two dozen colonies of emperor penguins have so far been

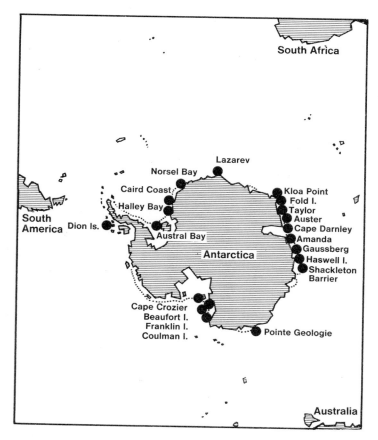

Known colonies of Emperor Penguins

17

First autumn arrivals on the newly formed sea ice, Adélie Land

discovered along the Antarctic coast, and biologists have lived among the birds of four of them. Only two colonies are on solid ground, the rest are on sea ice – which is probably warmer than rock in winter, because of the unfrozen sea below. Emperors breed in winter, brooding their eggs and chicks through the coldest months of the Southern continent – July and August when air temperatures fall to −40°C and lower. Wintering with emperors is a chilly but fascinating experience, for these curious birds, with breeding habits 'eccentric to a degree rarely met with even in ornithology', as their first investigator wrote, have much to teach us about how animals survive in an extreme climate.

Autumn gathering

March marks the end of summer in coastal Antarctica. Temperatures fall as the days shorten, winds blow colder from the continental slopes, and the sea surface thickens with the first ice of autumn. Most penguins have completed their breeding, and all the small species of coastal and peripheral Antarctica – Adélies, chinstraps, gentoos and macaronis – move out northwards towards the pack ice and warmer waters beyond. Here they can ride the floes and continue to feed throughout winter in a climate tempered by the presence of open water. Emperors alone head southwards over the newly-forming ice, swimming, waddling and tobogganing on shiny shirtfronts towards their traditional breeding areas. They travel in groups, pausing often to preen and to posture solemnly with melodious braying calls. Lone birds join the groups, one group merges with another, and all converge on the islet or patch of stable ice which will be their home for the winter. Like other mariners they probably navigate by the sun, recognising landmarks as they approach home. Many colonies form near prominent rocky massifs or headlands which can be seen from a distance.

At Pointe Géologie in Adélie Land, where twelve thousand emperors breed, the first birds appear in early March, still in the final stages of autumn moult. By late March nearly half the colony has assembled, and the young sea ice groans and bows under their accumulated weight. By early April all the breeding birds are present and courtship has begun. But violent winds in late March or April can disperse both the sea ice and the early birds several times before breeding begins; thus the start of the season can vary from year to year and from place to place.

The sexes are superficially alike, but at this stage of the annual cycle males are consistently heavier, averaging 76 lb. to the female's 58 lb. Males are noisier too, braying with prolonged, organ-like cadences which the females answer with short antiphonal calls.

Courtship and laying

We do not know if individuals seek and mate with their partner of the previous year. Penguins of several other species are known to re-mate often though not always but reunions usually occur at the previous year's nest site, to which both have returned at about the same time. Emperors might be expected to change partners more often, for their courtship involves much wandering and roaming through the colony. Yet on first arriving at the assembly in autumn both males and females give an impression of calling and listening, of ignoring or rejecting many replies to their calls, and accepting a particular response with excitement and satisfaction. Calls could therefore be their means of identifying an earlier partner, and retaining the pair bond for a further year. Later in courtship they call frequently as they lead and follow each other about the colony, perhaps reinforcing and relearning the recognition signals. The golden ear patches and black head plumage flash strikingly during courtship walks, and may play an important part in attracting breeding adults to each other.

A column of Emperors walking to the breeding area

*Newly arrived birds pairing up
at the nesting ground*

Copulation is hazardous in crowded colonies. The male mounts precariously on the female's back and treads warily, gripping her plumage with his long claws and trying hard, with bill and flippers, to steady himself on the slippery convex surface. Both are rotund as barrels in their pre-breeding fat. Left to themselves they are usually successful, but often wandering birds or neighbouring pairs crowd round and interfere, like an over-enthusiastic watch committee. Then the partners have to defend their activities against a jostling mob. This curious behaviour is not uncommon among colonial animals; it is probably evoked by the sign stimulus of the prone female, but seems to include mildly aggressive as well as sexual responses among bystanders. It must limit the number of successful copulations, and perhaps even restrict breeding in densely crowded colonies. Otherwise fighting and aggressive behaviour are rare, usually no more than jostling, pecking or lunging with the bill, and mild exchanges of flipper blows. The nonchalance of courting emperors contrasts sharply with the frenetic activity in Adélie and chinstrap colonies during the early stages of breeding.

Laying begins in May or June depending on the colonies. The single greenish-white eggs average 14–15 oz. each. Though large and robust in themselves, they represent a surprisingly small quantity of offspring from so large a bird. Eggs of some petrels may weigh as much as one seventh of adult weight, whereas those of emperors are only about one sixtieth of the weight of pre-breeding females. However, it is difficult to imagine emperors producing larger eggs without extensive modification of the anatomy of the pelvic region, and impossible to imagine them incubating two eggs by the method used for one. The male partner takes over the egg shortly after laying, and balances it carefully on the top of his broad, leathery feet. Then he settles gradually over it, retaining an upright posture but crouching with head and neck withdrawn. A fold of feathered skin with a warm, bare brood-patch drapes over the egg, and incubation begins. From time to time both parents examine the egg, calling repeatedly and pointing with their bills towards the brood cavity.

After a few minutes or hours the female loses interest and wanders off to join others of her kind whose partners have begun to incubate. Finally, and usually within half a day of laying, the females leave in groups for the sea, which by this time may be forty to sixty miles away beyond the northern horizon. Their partners now settle into the task of incubation which will occupy them without respite for two months.

A courting pair of Emperors

Why winter breeding?

Autumn courtship, winter incubation, and the curiously unequal division of responsibility between the parents, are the stratagems by which emperor penguins contrive to live in Antarctica. Desperate though they may seem, they are perfectly reasonable solutions to an ecological problem imposed by the size and length of the breeding cycle of the species. A fully grown emperor weighs over five times as much as Adélie, chinstrap and gentoo penguins, and seven to eight times as much as macaronis, the smallest Antarctic species. Emperor eggs take almost twice as long as the smaller species to incubate, and their chicks take over twice as long to reach independence. While the smaller species are able each year to fit courtship, incubation, chick-rearing and a post-breeding moult into five summer months from October to February, emperors barely manage to squeeze the same sequence into nine months. So their breeding fits incongruously across the highly seasonal Antarctic year.

Part of a huge huddle
of incubating male Emperors
in midwinter

The adults call and the young respond

Summer is, of course, the period of best weather, and therefore most favourable to incubating parents and growing chicks. More important, it is the time of year when food is abundant in the surface waters of the ocean. Not only is the sea ice-blanketed in winter, but many of the animals – planktonic crustacea and larval fish, probably also squid and larger fish – which make up the food of penguins descend into deep water between late April and September. Summer is therefore the only time when the ever-increasing food demands of growing chicks can be met satisfactorily. Emperor chicks hatching in December, like Adélies, would be making their greatest demands for food in April, May and June, when food is increasingly hard to catch and the climate is deteriorating rapidly towards winter. Instead, emperors must lay in May and incubate through the worst months of winter, so that the greatest demands of their growing chicks can be met in summer, when food is again plentiful at the surface.

Winter breeding imposes two major problems. Firstly, the weather is appalling, with temperatures often between −20°C and −40°C, strong winds and drifting snow, and little or no sunshine; at the southernmost colonies, e.g. Cape Crozier, only 900 miles from the South Pole, there is daylight for only one or two hours per day across midwinter. Secondly, food is virtually inaccessible from the colony areas, because an almost unbroken sheet of ice may extend for many miles from the coast, requiring a long and difficult journey to open water. Thus penguins attempting to breed in winter must be well equipped to avoid crippling heat losses, and able to live without food for long periods.

In both respects emperors are a match for the Antarctic winter. Like all other warm-blooded aquatic animals they are well insulated for their life in cold water, and the same mechanisms serve them well on land. Penguin plumage is a dense, overall cover, waterproof and virtually windproof. On every square inch of an emperor's body there are 70–80 stout feathers, each over one and a half inches long; beneath lies a layer of soft, dense underdown, which traps warm air close to the skin. Under this resilient and well-lined overcoat is a layer of fat up to three-quarters of an inch thick, permeated with fine blood-vessels which control its insulating qualities.

In sunshine – and even the weak, diffuse sunshine of the polar spring is effective – both dark dorsal and pale ventral feathers are readily warmed by solar energy, reducing any tendency for heat to flow outward from the penguin's body. The short bill, feet and flippers are further adaptations to reduce heat losses. For some purposes emperors are almost too well insulated. On clear sunny days in summer they have to pant and eat snow copiously to keep cool; even in winter a scurrying emperor overheats rapidly and must take time off to cool down. The solemn, imperial deportment of emperors probably reflects the efficiency of their insulation; whatever happens, an emperor must keep his cool.

Huddling

Incubating and brooding birds spend much of their winter asleep, packed tightly together in huddles. A single huddle may include several thousands of sleepy birds, who jostle quietly for a position well inside the pack, grumble gently to each other and snore unromantically in the cold air. In bad weather the huddles remain intact for days on end. In fine weather they break; the birds preen,

A huddle of chicks in early spring

23

*Well-grown chicks
at the Cape Crozier colony*

yawn and stretch, shuffling slowly over the ice with the eggs cradled safely on their feet. They scratch acrobatically with one foot, balancing the egg on the other, posture to themselves and their neighbours, check their eggs myopically, and call braying messages through the winter twilight. Then the huddles re-form and lethargy settles again.

Huddling is a simple expedient which helps emperors to exist with the minimum of energy expenditure. Incubating emperors held for experiment in solitary confinement on the colony were found to use about three-quarters of a pound of fat per day to maintain body temperature against the extreme cold. Huddling birds under similar conditions lost only a little over one-quarter of a pound per day. Only by huddling can emperors mete out their food reserves during the long fast required by courtship and incubation. Packing tightly together reduces the effective surface area of each bird by about 80 per cent. There is some evidence that huddling birds are able to reduce their body temperature by a few degrees, thus lowering the temperature gradient between themselves and the environment, and helping to minimise heat losses.

A more orthodox pattern of incubation, in which the two parents took short spells of incubation and continually crossed the ice from colony to open water, would involve both of them in considerable expenditure of energy at the very time when food

24

is hard to get and energy cannot readily be replaced. Thus the male emperors' assumption of full responsibility for incubation is by far the most economical method of getting the job done. Though their fasting may extend over three months or more from the start of courtship to the return of their partner, they seem well able to cope at every stage, and are far from exhausted when their annual ordeal is over.

Most Emperors never come to land, spending their entire lives at sea or on sea-ice

Hatching and growth

During the final days of incubation the first returning females invade the club-like atmosphere of the huddles. Clean, lively, and very much fatter than the males at this stage, they bring an air of excitement, a breath of the outside world coupled with a strong smell of part-digested fish. They barge through groups of protesting, sleepy males, calling repeatedly in quest of their families. Finding the right partner, each female recovers her egg and settles immediately to incubate. As more and more females pour in, a growing stream of males leaves the colony for the open sea, which may by this time be visible on the northern horizon. Then a new sound is heared – the shrill piping of hatching chicks, and soon the colony floor is littered with discarded shells and egg membranes. The chicks, silver-grey with black heads and watery black eyes, take the place of the egg on their parents' feet.

Returning females bring with them a cropful of food – partly digested fish and squid – which they feed to the chicks by regurgitation from their crop. Males whose partners are late in arriving produce a crop secretion, similar in composition to pigeons' milk, which helps to tide the chicks over for a few days.

For the first three or four weeks of its life the chick is fed every few hours by its mother. Emperor chicks grow very slowly during these first weeks. Adélie or gentoo chicks double their hatching weight in three to four days, but emperors take four times as long; Adélies reach ten times their hatching weight in two weeks, while emperors take nearly three months.

The chicks remain on the parents' feet for seven to eight weeks, fattening steadily and gradually acquiring the ability to maintain their own body temperature. After the first return of the males, the two parents alternate more often, and rates of feeding and growth begin to accelerate. At eight weeks the chicks stand sturdily on their own feet and group together in nurseries or crèches, leaving both parents free to search for food. Though the surface waters are still icebound and impoverished, cracks and open lakes are appearing closer to the colony, and longer hours of daylight help the parents in their search for food at depth. On returning to the colony, the parent calls from the edge of the crèche, and its own chick responds with frantic whistles from the middle of the group.

Young chick imprisoned in a crevasse

By late October the chicks are receiving one-third of their own weight in food every second or third day and stowing it in aldermanic paunches. By late November they begin to lose their grey woolly down, and December and January see them shedding their down altogether and emerging as small replicas of their parents. The bill plates are dark and leathery. The full glory of adult colouring is probably not achieved until their second summer.

Now the sea ice breaks up and floats northwards to join the slowly swirling pack. The juveniles are literally launched, with the balance of the summer before them, to fend for themselves and continue growing during the months of richest feeding. Relieved of responsibility at last, the hard-working parents also fatten and moult while food is still plentiful.

Early visitors to the Cape Crozier colony, where emperors were first studied over fifty years ago, found it difficult to believe that animals could normally subject themselves to the rigours of the Antarctic winter, and were not surprised to find a very heavy mortality of eggs and chicks. We now know that the colony was then passing through a difficult phase, due to changes in the face of the Ross Ice Shelf which had left it vulnerable to storm damage in early winter. Studies at Cape Crozier and other colonies since then have shown that the winter breeding of emperors is no more hazardous than the summer breeding of other species. Few adults

Emperor chicks panting
in the sub-zero temperature

27

On land Emperors progress either by walking or 'tobogganing'

are reported to die in the colonies in winter; males are probably safer sleeping the winter away in their clubs than exposing themselves to the dangers of winter fishing. Losses of eggs and chicks usually vary between 20 per cent and 50 per cent up to fledging. Generally more chicks than eggs are lost, from a combination of starvation and cold, and a single heavy blizzard or snowfall late in the year can play havoc with a crop of otherwise healthy chicks. However, much the same is true of summer-breeding species, whose losses and causes of loss are very similar.

So in spite of the seeming eccentricity of their breeding behaviour, emperors are as successful, flourishing and essentially normal a group of birds as one could meet. It would be difficult to think of an easier or more economical solution to the biological problems which face them; natural selection has – as always – provided the best, and the best, as usual, has the quality of inventiveness which is every naturalist's delight.

The Siamese Fighting Fish   *Michael Simpson*

It is always a surprise to find that so little is known of the life in the wild of a species so widely domesticated. Yet although *Betta splendens* ('betta' to aquarists) abounds in the slow weedy streams and irrigation ditches near Bangkok in Thailand, and in the paddy fields of Malaya, much more is known about the various domesticated forms than about the original wild stock. At present we must use the studies of captive fish to fill in our picture of the lives of the wild fish. Bettas are among the most popular freshwater aquarium fishes, and in Bangkok they are bred so that fights between the males can be staged for betting. Because this is illegal it is more difficult to see than before. In the West betta is an ornamental pet, the males having long flowing fins, and is bred in such plastic-bright colours as lavender, maroon, emerald, cobalt and pink. The females of the ornamental breed have remained more like the wild ones, their fins being quite short. Bettas are also widely used in laboratories, being almost as phlegmatic as laboratory rats. A wild betta, in contrast, is timid and apt to start out of his tank at any sudden movement.

The wild fish

One's first view is often a disappointment. Drab, olive-coloured fish, with two dark stripes along their bodies (indicating fear), they usually skulk on the bottom of their tank. The males' pelvic and ventral fins, unlike those of the ornamental ones, are only slightly longer than those of the females. Every minute or so, one inches up through the weed to gulp air from the surface, then darts back down. As a member of the Anabantidae family of fish, a betta can breathe air directly, which he passes back into special labyrinthine chambers above the gill cavities. In their poorly aerated, stagnant home streams, these fish must often get all their oxygen from the air.

The wild fish feed mainly on insect larvae, especially of the mosquito, which is also the main food given to the Bangkok fighting breeds. Ornamental fish are more often fed on *Tubifex* worms, and doubtless the wild fish eat bottom-living worms as well as insect larvae.

In the natural condition these fish probably breed all the year round. Some of the adult males will be defending territories. In these they build florin-sized, floating, domed nests out of saliva-

Wild Siamese fighting fish abound in thickly weeded streams in the Far East – such as the one above near Bangkok in Thailand

coated bubbles, moored to a piece of weed. As an air-breather, the species is well adapted to making such nests. Under the nests spawning takes place, and the eggs are then placed up in the dome and are there looked after by the males.

The male defends the area within six or nine inches of the nest against all other bettas, except ripe females. Territory-owning males are strikingly different from non-breeding fish. Their bodies are dark velvety crimson, jewelled with turquoise on the scale-centres and on the eyes, and barred scarlet and old gold on the gill covers. The fins are also crimson, with bright green streaks between the rays (though a fright will within seconds cause the males to revert to the drab-olive-plus-two-longitudinal-stripes pattern, but again, at the sight of an intruding male, the fish will as quickly reassume his bright colours!). His behaviour also advertises his presence in his territory – he patrols its boundaries, swimming fast yet deliberately, with all his fins spread, and his tail flashing bright green as it closes and opens like a fan.

It is seldom possible to arrange for ornamental bettas to share out even a large tank into separate territories, unless they have been there together from birth. An ornamental male introduced to a new tank is usually intolerant of any other male betta. This may be an effect of the isolation aquarists usually enforce on their fish, in order to protect their long fins, and it may also be a difference of strain between the wild and ornamental fish. But it is with reference to the latter, the ornamental betta, that I shall describe the social behaviour involved in setting up and defending territories, how the males induce females to come under their nests, and how a male and female co-operate in spawning. But first, what of man's earliest interest in bettas?

Betting on fights between the males

A Victorian ichthyologist and theologian, Theodore Cantor, wrote in 1849 that 'the Siamese are infatuated with the combats of these fishes as the Malays are with their cock fights, and stake considerable sums and sometimes their own persons and their families.' The fish he described then were probably trapped wild males. In 1939, according to H. M. Smith, advising the Siam Government in Fisheries, noteworthy combats were by then with selected, often pedigreed, stock. Professionals never bred from losing fish. Such selection for fighting, therefore, may have started sometime within the last hundred years. Like so many male animals which have been isolated beforehand, and which have not seen each other before, two males (domesticated or wild) will fight when put into the same container. These fights are at first mainly displays, and in the *wild* fish they may end soon, without any bites being exchanged, or after fifteen minutes at most. The loser is the one who first folds his fins, begins to avoid the other, and shows the longitudinal 'fear' stripes. In a natural situation, the winner then has first access to local territory, food sources and so on, and the loser goes elsewhere. In a confined situation, the winner may continue to chase and harass the loser.

Fights between fish specially bred for the purpose may last as long as six hours, and those that fail to fight for longer than one hour are regarded as failures. The fighting breed resembles the wild one in having rather short fins and tails for their darting sparring movements, and for avoiding the extensive fin tearing seen in the long-finned ornamental breeds, some of which also fight hard and long. It is perhaps because the outcome of these fights is so difficult for people to predict, that they have remained

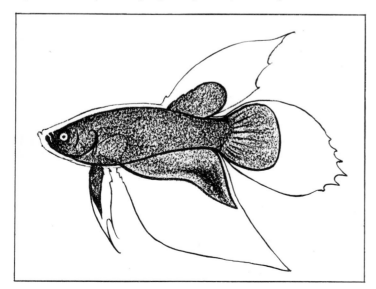

Drawing to show comparative structures of the wild and ornamental male Siamese fighting fish. The wild species (shaded) is smaller with less developed pelvic, ventral, caudal and dorsal fins

such popular subjects for wagers. Do we know enough about what the fish do to each other during their encounters to predict the outcome? Can we make a lot of money? In other words, what does a fish have to do to win?

But first, what purpose in the lives of the *wild* fish could such elaborate displays and fights have? They are a way in which a fish's status, in terms of whether it has access to a particular area or not, is determined. This is necessary when two fish come upon one area new to both, as must happen when breeding areas are limited. Although the displays may be prolonged, they often end without damage to either rival. The dispute starts gently and 'escalates' until the loser gives up. Thus the final intensity of the fight is determined by the least aggressive of the two, so that the outcome is decided with the minimum of effort to both. Often one of the two is already established in his territory, and the other is a trespassing stranger. Then the established fish almost always wins, and the stranger moves on to display with the other established fish in the area, thereby learning the extent of their territories. Displays between the resident neighbours are very brief – a glance by one often sufficing to check and remind its intruding neighbour.

How does one fish win in a situation where neither has the advantage of already owning territory? When the fight continues until both bite in earnest, it is usually the individual that bites most who wins. More interesting, however, are the fights where the outcome is decided *without* many bites being exchanged – without, as it were, coming to blows. Then it must be by the pattern of their displays, rather than brute force, that the fish show each other which *could* bite most, were they to begin in earnest. So it is worth looking for differences between the displays of the two rivals, and seeing if such differences are related to outcome. But first, what are the basic moves in the display?

Few animals could provide more vivid examples of what a display is than do the ornamental fighting fish. Their fins are stretched taut, the colours deepen and brighten and shimmer, the red and gold-slashed gill covers are raised, and the sooty-black and red underlying membranes spread in a dragon-like ruff. But 'display' gives the wrong impression – of a static show. The fishes' movements are as formal and co-ordinated as ballet, one fish facing and the other blocking the first by presenting his broadside. Then the first turns broadside, and the second turns to face. Thus they may face each other in turn, perhaps six or ten times every minute. The two seldom face each other at once, but they often stand parallel, broadside to broadside, and they sometimes move along thus, bumping and boring like schoolboys in a corridor.

By such movements the fishes ritualise their moment-by-moment readiness to attack each other, without actually attacking. Thus a fish shows readiness to advance by turning to face its partner without actually moving nearer, and it adds emphasis by folding back

Male chasing female away from nest prior to mating

Clasping

The white dots on the male's tail are the falling eggs

The female lying motionless on her side while the male chases for eggs

An ornamental male chasing for eggs which he will place in the nest

A red ornamental male

A green ornamental male

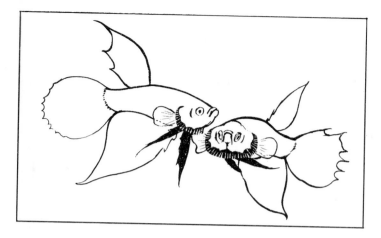

Courtship display of the ornamental fighting fish. Their fins are stretched taut, their colours deepen, the gill covers are raised and the underlying membranes ruffed out

its paired pelvic fins, a thing fish usually do when they start to move forwards. In returning to the broadside position, the fish re-erects its pelvic fins, as does a fish when braking to a halt, and in the context of the display it thus shows that it is standing its ground. The broadside fish may add emphasis by flickering to and fro the pelvic fin on the side away from the partner, soon after it has turned broadside. This interpretation is confirmed by the fact that the more aggressive fish, in a situation where they display to a standard stationary puppet fish, are those which flicker their pelvic fins most, and face for longest.

The display is also ritualised in the sense that there are conventions which prevent mutual damage. Thus, when one fish stops displaying to gulp air, the other does likewise. When the two circle each other slowly in a head-to-tail carousel position, movement of one's head closer than a quarter of an inch from the other's tail is checked by a quick closing and opening of the other's tail. Before the fish actually bite each other, they merely open their mouths near their partners' gill covers and heads, and their first few bites go past the hind ends of the partners' fins.

Often an encounter ends after several tail beats and only a few bites have been exchanged. What are the differences between the displays of winner- and loser-to-be? The most impressive thing about the display is the way in which the behaviour of the partners is matched. In addition to facing in turn, they may exchange tail beat for tail beat, and bite for bite. And, as one faces with its gill covers erect for longer, so will the partner, when his turn comes. Perhaps there is never any difference between the two, and the loser is simply the fish that gets tired first. But a loser in one encounter can at once start up with another fish, and beat it as often as not.

While the displays of two fish are at first rather perfectly matched, towards the end a difference does emerge – the winner-to-be holds his gill covers erect for longer periods of time than his partner. Up to then, each fish has prevented his partner's gill cover erections lasting more than a few seconds by beating his tail. Eventually, however, the loser's tail-beating fails to prevent the winner from raising its gill covers for longer. Thus, when a display stops, it does so because the loser responds to quite a complex situation: the difference between its own gill cover erections and those of its partner. Small wonder that it is difficult to predict the outcome of such intricate displays. It is tempting to compare such an interaction with many of the games played by human beings. Thus this particular game is played only when the result is not foregone, when the fish are strangers to each other. There is also a sense in which the fish enjoy displaying. Professor Thompson has shown that a chance to display rewards learning – bettas will learn to swim through a hoop if the consequence is a view of a puppet, or their own mirror image, at which they can display.

Courtship and spawning

In paradoxical contrast to the displays between males, which start like gentlemanly games, the first stages of courtship are often violent. Success in courtship depends on the male learning to tolerate the female near his nest, and both must come into sufficient rapport for the co-operation required in spawning. This may take as little as an hour, or as long as forty-eight. Because 'matches' between the fish are so often unsuccessful, and even when successful so variable in how long they take to consummate, breeding ornamental bettas can be as exciting a gamble for aquarists as betting on fights used to be for the people in the Bangkok bars.

In wild bettas, courtship sometimes starts when a male goes outside his territory to seek out a female lurking in the weeds, sometimes, when a female swims into his territory. A ripe female has a bulging silvery-gold belly, and when she sees the male, she swims directly towards him, spreads her fins and gill covers, and then swims away with stiff, mincing movements. If an aquarist introduces a ripe female into a male's tank, her initial fear stripes

An ornamental male Siamese fighting fish with a female

34

The female fighting fish recognised by the less developed fins

are soon overlaid and then replaced by vertical golden stripes, which also appear on ripe wild females when they see a male.

The male raises his gill covers and faces her, as if doubtful whether to treat her as an intruder. Then he rushes away, all his fins spread, and zigzags all over his territory. She follows, often in his exact path. At first both swim straight by the nest, then the male pauses when he passes under it, but he leaves as the female approaches, as if he is frightened as well as excited by her. Over the first few minutes of courtship the male may allow the female near the nest for longer, but never does he stay near her for more than a few seconds. She soon begins to explore in his territory on her own, and he may add more bubbles to his nest.

When one begins to hope that the male will allow the female nearby for longer, he suddenly turns on her and chases her, often ramming her hard as she dives into the thickest clump of weed. There she hides motionless, except to lift her head to take air. Although chased thus, a ripe female remains in the male's territory, without fleeing right away as would one not fully ripe. The male is beginning to accept her, in so far as he has not hounded her right out of his territory.

The female remains out of sight and unvisited by the male for perhaps a further quarter of an hour. Then his approaches to the female's hiding place are brief, and each time he comes near he quickly turns broadside and, after briefly flickering his pelvic fins and beating his tail, he swims zigzag back to the nest, his tail flashing green. At first the female follows him a little way only, or not at all, but as he repeats his visits every minute or so, she follows further. Eventually (sometimes after as long as forty-eight hours) both are swimming around under the nest, apparently more at ease with each other.

As in the courtship of so many animals, getting to know each other has involved each becoming less fearful of and aggressive towards the other. Such fear and aggression can prevent the close co-operation required for the subsequent spawning. A betta female will not spawn until she is clasped between the male's cheek and tail – the male's body bent over and wrapped round the upside-down female in an arch, so that the eggs can be fertilised as they are laid and fall past his genital pore and into his ventral fin, which is folded on to the female. About twenty eggs are laid per clasp, and after each clasp the male gathers them in his mouth and places them in the nest, until about two hundred (usually) or as many as seven hundred have been laid. By receiving and fertilising the eggs in batches of about twenty, the male is able to gather and place them as they are laid. If he attempted to manage all two hundred at once, most would drift away as he placed the first mouthful of twenty or so.

The precise yet flowing movements of a spawning couple beggar written descriptions, so that, in comparison to reality, they read like earnest marriage manuals. Both sexes contribute equally in a successful clasp, so that it is hardly possible to refer to either as the more active partner, as one can in the brute ruttings of so many land animals. For such reasons, perhaps, we find the spawning so pleasing to watch.

Clasping is repeated until all the eggs are laid, and very soon after the first clasp without eggs the male chases the female away, and hounds her well out of his territory.

Now he frequently mouths the eggs, removing and replacing them attached to fresh bubbles, and then pushing them further up into the dome of the nest, which he builds up by adding new bubbles underneath. The eggs hatch after about three days, and the fry are at first denser than water, and those that drop out sink headfirst to the bottom. When the fry swim, they can at first only go vertically upwards until they hit the surface, where they skid around at random until retrieved by the male. He also searches the bottom for young, fanning it and picking up those that are swept into view. He spits them out just under the nest, and they stick as they hit it.

By about four days after hatching, the babies' swim-bladders fill with air, and they can then swim at all levels in the water. Although they are only the size of small pin-heads, they already have developed jaws and eyes, and they fixate and engulf appropriate microscopic creatures, one at a time. By this time the male loses interest in the nest and the babies, and he may now eat any he finds. They disperse, and in about a hundred days the males among them will be building their own first nests.

How long does a Siamese fighter live?

How long a wild Siamese Fighter might live is not known. In captivity, a fish-keeper will tell you that of all the commonly kept 'tropicals' the Siamese Fighter lives for the shortest time. Two years is a very good life, and two-and-a-half years exceptional. Thus if the fish matures at six months it is in real splendour for a year at the most, after which it begins noticeably to age.

This sketch is an attempt by a scientist to share with the reader the effort to understand a few aspects of the behaviour of Siamese Fighting Fish. A few outlines of the aquarium breeds' private lives are there, enabling us to make guesses about what the wild fish do. But why do bettas fascinate their owners so? A written account can only hint at the vividness of these fishes' fighting and court-ship behaviour, which must surely provide rich material for our own private wishes and dreams.

The Red Fox   *Roger Burrows*

*Defensive attitude with
ears well back and mouth open
to display an impressive collection
of teeth. Note the large stabbing
canines near the front of the jaw
and the shearing teeth further back*

Some foxes live in fables, in country pub stories, Hunt Ball discussions and old natural history books. Real foxes live in earths and their private lives are quite different. Each red fox (*Vulpes vulpes*) spends much of its time avoiding other foxes by a variety of scent and vocal mechanisms. Foxes certainly keep in touch but by 'bush telegraph' rather than the social gathering. Only the necessity to reproduce the species brings them together, and then for a few weeks at the most. Domestic life is probably almost unknown to the adult dog fox and the family unit is made up of vixen and cubs with rarely if ever a visit from father.

A young fox's solitary existence starts in the autumn following its birth in the previous spring. In autumn young foxes can be seen, long-legged and thin-brushed, making use of twilight hours for scavenging the easily obtained meal from orchard, dustbin, compost heap or slug-infested kale crop. They will eat what is most readily and easily obtained and nothing seems to be missed.

Young dog foxes travel far from their birthplaces in their first winter, and it is in the winter months that there are reports of giant 'bags' of foxes. Thirty to forty have been killed on a few acres but this only represents a moving population, mainly of dog foxes, and should not be taken as evidence of a fox invasion, as it so often is. Well-padded trails at this time are not an indication of foxes hunting in packs but only evidence of moving foxes using the same trails at different times.

Winter activity

In the winter months the young fox will find that most of the areas through which he passes already have a resident barking male fox population which will hardly welcome the young dog's presence. Early winter brings banshee-like yells and screams heard over the wind of a winter gale or during the still of a frosty moonlit night, for it is then that the foxes vocally begin to assert their seasonal territorial claims. Vocal combats can probably explain many stories of Hallowe'en witches whose supposed yells could be traced to a vulpine rather than a satanic source. Little blood is shed in normal fox disputes as the strength of the yells and the persistence and aggressive attitudes of the resident seem to unnerve the intruding vocal adversary. The stranger moves on.

Vocal contests seem partly to decide the 'pecking order' of the

local resident fox population which, in an area of a few hundred acres, may contain two dogs with a similar or probably larger number of resident vixens. Population density is of course variable but may be anything from one to twenty foxes per square mile.

Our wandering young dog fox leaves the area to the residents who now in early winter begin the preliminaries of the breeding season. Vixens in autumn clear out the earths used for their last litter and leave a characteristic 'trade-mark' in the form of a dropping on the newly excavated earth. The earths themselves are usually secondhand, borrowed temporarily from rabbit or badger. Having selected a suitable earth the vixen then lives in this during the winter days. Dog foxes seldom use the relative comfort of an earth, preferring to lie up on the surface.

By December the scenting routine can be smelt by even a keen city nose as a rank mustiness hanging fitfully in moist morning air. The fox 'scents' by rubbing a secretion from its anal glands on suitable projecting parts of its environment. Sometimes the fox will thresh a small bush or clump of herbs with its tail, presumably by this means dispersing the scent on the foliage; it will also roll on the freshly scented areas. Urination is used to mark projecting stumps of trees or mounds of fresh earth. In snow the yellow urine stains can be seen near almost anything that breaks through the snow blanket and twenty to thirty urination points in as many yards are not uncommon. Foxes will urinate or defecate at the spot where they ate a meal and will 'decorate' any left-overs with a dropping. In the bad days of gin traps the fox had many a meal of trapped rabbit and, as is its habit, left behind a urine smell or a dropping. This was taken to be a mark of the fox's disdain for the poor human who tried to catch this creature of such supposed cunning and intelligence. When, however, the event is viewed in the light of a fox's normal activities after a meal, such a sophisticated explanation is unnecessary.

Vocal 'combat' may result in the rapid flight of the loser. An American red fox in full gallop

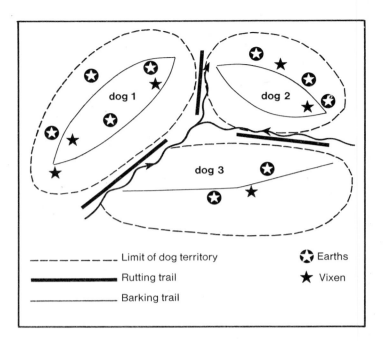

*Diagram of three dog fox territories
bounded, in this case, by small streams.
Maximum distance across the territories
about $\frac{1}{4}$ to $\frac{1}{2}$ a mile.
(Based on the author's work
in Gloucestershire)*

---------- Limit of dog territory   ✪ Earths

▬▬▬▬ Rutting trail   ★ Vixen

─────── Barking trail

Territory

By the scenting mechanisms the fox seems to mark out an area of
land that we call its territory and in which it is supreme. To what
extent a fox holds a territory permanently is not known for certain.
The vixen, or vixens, living in a dog fox's territory do so, it seems,
throughout their lives, until death makes room for a young vixen
of the new season's litter. Fox mortality by various artificial
means is so high, probably near 100,000 per year in the British
Isles, that it is unnecessary for a young female to move far from her
birth area. In areas where foxes are regularly dug out in spring, the
vixen's expectation of life is seldom more than two years.

The vixen society is a loose one; a number of individuals use the
same hunting area, but at different times, so avoiding direct
confrontations. Chance encounters are probably settled by vocal
means and a fairly stable hierarchy is established. Vixens scent-
mark as do the dogs, but their scenting activity is probably more
concerned with social status than with territorial ambition. Some
vixens form small close communities during the cubs' early
weeks, and three litters under one Worcestershire pig house were
discovered a few years ago.

In December and January the dog is roused to announce his
territorial claim to the vixens by a typical winter bark which is a
double or triple *wo-wo*, repeated sometimes at regular intervals
as the dog patrols his bounds. His barking trail is roughly the same
each evening and he is at his vocal best just after nightfall. By

An earth in an old hayrick.
A most unusual site
but the adaptable fox will use
many man-provided covers including
a cricket pavilion loft
and the basement of a pig-house

regular listening it is possible to recognise the voices of dog foxes occupying adjacent areas, as the barks vary both in pitch and in the number of *wo-wo's* used.

Mating

Most vixens come into heat in January, although earlier and much later matings are by no means uncommon. At this time the dog fox can often be seen wandering about in daylight, particularly in the early morning as he returns home from his matrimonial involvement, for even at this time the pairs do not cohabit. Pairs are also frequently seen performing stiff-legged, high-leaping dances around one another, sometimes in silence or with a shrieking vocal backing. This dance seems to precede copulation. The resident dog probably fathers the cubs of all the vixens in his territory although further confirmation of this polygamous behaviour is needed.

After insemination the female no longer accepts the attention of the male who soon ceases to bark, and the scenting activity declines until by the end of February it is difficult to find any 'sign' in the area that a few weeks earlier had reeked of fox. The whole tempo of fox life slackens and the dog foxes seem almost to vanish. What they do with themselves after mating is still a mystery.

Cubs

Litters of fox cubs have been found during most months of the year, their birth date being about fifty-two days after conception.

The vixen provides no bedding
for her cubs who are kept warm
by the woolly black fur
with which they are born.
Note the white tip to the cub's tail.
The vixen suckles her cubs underground
for the first few weeks of their lives.
The photograph shows an American red
fox which is thought to be the
same species as the European red fox

In the British Isles most cubs are born in late March or April, the earlier births taking place in the south. Cubs are born with a fine black fur, a necessary clothing when it is remembered that the vixen provides no bedding material for her offspring. Litters vary from one to six or sometimes more but the average is between four and five.

Vixens suckle their cubs below ground and kennel with them for about four weeks, leaving their earths during April just after sunset to forage. After four weeks the woolly, black cubs, tails tipped with white, begin to explore the entrance to their earth. If the vixen suspects human presence she lightly hiccups down the tunnel and no cubs will be seen that night. If she has no sensory knowledge of human danger the cubs will emerge soon after their mother and play, kitten-like, around the earth.

After the first month of the cubs' life the vixen ceases to kennel with her litter, preferring to lie up at some little distance from the earth and visit her family at fairly regular intervals.

In May visits occur just after sunrise, again in mid-afternoon, and finally early evening. The daytime feeds are brief; the cubs usually greet the vixen a few yards from the earth. It is very rare to see prey being brought to them and the vixen may regurgitate food to the cubs after they have been suckled. Eric Ashby has filmed two vixens in the New Forest feeding one litter.

42

A vixen in May hunts in full mid-afternoon sun, often passing unseen near men working in gardens or fields. She approaches her cubs boldly without taking circuitous routes, but should she be disturbed will gallop silently away without warning the cubs of human presence. If the vixen detects human scent in the evening visit, however, she gives a series of loud *woooohs*. These single shrieks rise at the end to a high pitch, to be repeated a few seconds later. Such sounds inform the cubs of danger and they will usually retreat rapidly to the safety of their earth.

An evening vixen visit is the most exciting to watch, and provided a suitable observation post is taken up well before the fox's arrival, in a spot where human scent will not reach the sensitive moist nose, many unforgettable observations can be made. The vixen approaches silently and is quickly surrounded by a leaping, snapping family who have been awaiting her arrival for some time. She may sit for a few minutes with her family but is soon on the move again, taking the cubs some little distance from the earth for the evening romp. Cubs' play is fast and at times furious as they leap at one another from behind trees or charge headlong through tall mowing grass. The episode is short, however, for the vixen will soon bring the family back to the earth at a gallop. Now about six weeks old, cubs are becoming much more fox-like and growing the typical reddish coat, often with a vivid blaze on the tip of the brush. This latter feature is a tremendous aid to fox-watching in poor light.

It is popularly supposed that the vixen will teach her cubs how to catch prey and that she will bury prey so that the cubs can learn to use their noses to discover food. This seems to be one of the many fox myths. From analysis of the cubs' droppings it is

Twelve-day-old cub two days after the eyes first open

Cubs about eight weeks old. They can be seen outside the earths on most sunny days in May

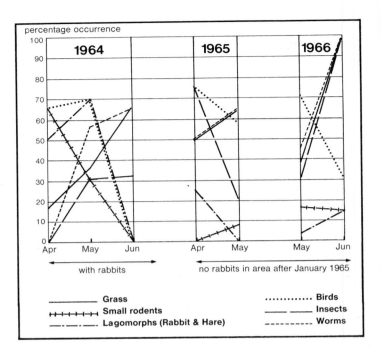

percentage occurrence

1964 1965 1966

Apr May Jun   Apr May   May Jun

with rabbits   no rabbits in area after January 1965

————— Grass   ·············· Birds
+++++++ Small rodents   — — — Insects
—·—·—·— Lagomorphs (Rabbit & Hare)   - - - - - - Worms

*Cub diet, based on analysis
of droppings (scats) collected from
earths in lowland Gloucestershire,
and expressed as percentage
occurrence, which is:*

$$\frac{\text{number of times item found}}{\text{number of scats analysed}} \times 100$$

*Note how the larger items of prey,
such as birds and mammals,
tend to decrease as
the vixen ceases to feed the cubs*

obvious that in summer they are eating anything and everything
from beetles and worms to string, coal and even old rags. Just as
with many other animals the cubs have to find out for themselves
what is good to eat and what is not. Prey-burying is a normal
activity of foxes throughout the year if there is a food surplus.
Food so cached may be found by the cubs but it is very doubtful
whether the vixen intentionally buries it for educational purposes.

Having brought the cubs back to the earth the vixen, unless
suspecting human presence, will go off on her own to forage.
Should she get a whiff of human scent she will hiccup continuously a short distance from the earth to which the cubs will make a
rapid dive.

Foxes have few natural enemies in the British Isles but golden
eagles have been known to kill fox cubs and even to attack adults.
Badgers are sometimes accused of killing fox-cubs. There is little
direct evidence for this and on many occasions fox-cubs have been
seen playing on a badger set in which they have their home, the
resident badgers at least tolerating the intrusion.

Break-up of family life

In June the cubs leave the earths and take up residence in a nearby
hedge or dry ditch which gives suitable cover. They catch most
of their own invertebrate food, leaping cat-like for moths and
flying beetles in the warm late evenings. Cub play begins at sunset when loud shrieks, yaps and the characteristic *tak tak* note of

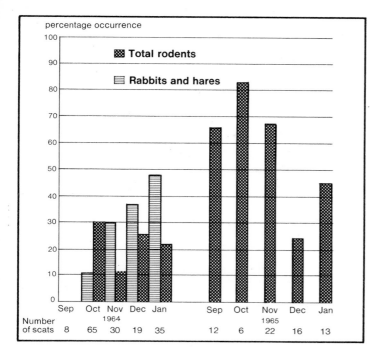

Number of scats	Sep 8	Oct 65	Nov 1964 30	Dec 19	Jan 35	Sep 12	Oct 6	Nov 1965 22	Dec 16	Jan 13

Diagram to show how the fox switched over to a diet of small rodents, mainly field voles, after myxomatosis had destroyed the local rabbit population in Gloucestershire. There was no increase in predation on domestic or farm animals

annoyance announces the onset of the night's activities. Vocal content in the play gradually becomes more prominent and play obviously more aggressive. Each night's watching brings more evidence of the far from playful nature of the hitherto 'mock' fights. With aggressive play the fox family begins to break up into twos and threes. By the end of August cubs are independent from, but still loosely associated with, their mother.

Warm full-moon nights in late summer seem to rouse foxes to utter ear-piercing yells which are similar to those given by the vixen as a long-range warning of danger. The exact significance of these yells is obscure but it may be that the adult fox population is now using them to discourage the cubs from settling down in that area, and to promote an exodus to pastures new. Certainly in August the adults begin their scenting routine and from September to November running fights can be followed by ear as fox pursues fox over the countryside uttering shrieking threats.

Young foxes may stay in twos until early winter when the young males begin their wanderings and leave their female litter-mates. These come on to heat after the older vixens in the home area and produce their first litter just over a year from their date of birth.

Food

The fox spends a great deal of its time avoiding direct confrontation with either other members of its own species or with man. A fox's very private life impinges on man's interests in one im-

45

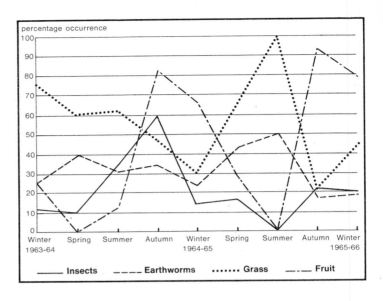

percentage occurrence

——— **Insects**   – – – **Earthworms**   ······· **Grass**   –·–· **Fruit**

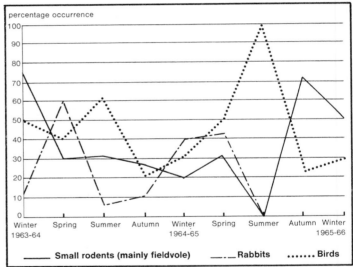

Adult fox diet. Seasonal fluctuations in the proportion of various major prey items.

——— **Small rodents (mainly fieldvole)**   –·–· **Rabbits**   ······· **Birds**

portant way and that is in its diet. But what does a fox really eat? Not all chickens, lambs and cats as is so commonly thought to be basic to their diet. Major items are field voles, beetles, earthworms, fruit, grass and other vegetation, and probably most important of all, carrion. There is much circumstantial, but almost no direct evidence to support the idea that foxes kill lambs, sheep or cats. Dead animals of any sort they will certainly take, and leave the remains outside their earths. Many a fox has been dug out and killed on the evidence of the remains of one or two still-born lambs outside its earth in spring. Investigators who have taken the trouble to find out how the lambs died have discovered that, in nearly all cases, death was due to natural causes at birth or starvation after birth.

If foxes are wrongly accused of lamb-slaughter the same cannot be said about fowl-killing. Chickens, ducks and occasionally geese are taken by foxes given the chance, but in these days of battery and broiler it is mainly the dead chickens thrown on to the rubbish heap that account for much domestic fowl in fox diet. Despite the availability of rats they seldom figure prominently in the diet. Occasionally one will be killed but it seems that most rats eaten by foxes are those killed by man's activity.

The fox is basically a rodent eater and scavenger and as such is a very useful member of our native fauna. Its prowess as a killer is wildly exaggerated and probably more money is spent in attempting to destroy foxes than the damage they do is worth.

Urban take-over

Of recent years foxes have taken up residence in highly urban areas and are now established animals in many towns and cities. Breeding foxes are reported from suburban council-house gardens where their presence has led to neighbours' feuds over the pros and cons of the animal. In Bristol, Plymouth and London early-morning fox-spotting expeditions have been arranged to try to establish just how common the fox is in suburbia.

Foxes have not only increased in towns but have been doing so

Domestic dogs are frequently seen playing with tame and sometimes with wild foxes. Mating has been reported between the two species but no offspring result

47

A fox being attacked by a hooded crow. This fox was observed at a lakeside in Finland where it would come in the early mornings and late evenings to feed on frog-spawn and pond snails. The various birds feeding in the vicinity showed little reaction to the fox, except for a few hooded crows who would mob it half-heartedly for a short time. The fox made no effort to stalk the birds

for many years in the countryside. Their numbers seem to have grown with the progressive destruction of the natural vegetation of the British Isles. In the days of the great deciduous forests foxes were not common, but as the trees fell and the land was given over to scrub and farms, so the fox multiplied. Unlike most mammals the fox can adapt to man's activities very easily. Man provides suitable places for earths in quarries, railway embankments, old marl-pits, overgrown ditches and golf courses, not to mention the earths actually constructed for them by fox hunters. Equally important, man produces abundant food.

In our 'effluent society' the fox seems to have an affluent future if urban man can learn to accept into his private life this much maligned and little understood mammal.

Vixen with four-day-old cubs

Five-week-old cubs beginning to get their adult red coats

Dog fox courting vixen. The vocal preliminaries to mating can be heard during January and February

The Kingfisher *Jeffery Boswall*

'The secret splendour of the brooks', Tennyson called it. Linnaeus dubbed it scientifically *Alcedo atthis,* after Alcyone who was the daughter of Aeolus, god of the winds, the Greek legend being that she was turned into the bird that afterwards bore her name. The term 'halcyon days' refers to the old belief that the bird made a floating nest on the sea, the water remaining calm while the eggs were being incubated.

These are but two of the many poetic allusions to the common kingfisher, the most brightly coloured bird in Britain. Its back is a dazzling blue, or it can look emerald green depending on the light. Underneath, the cock bird is a warm chestnut orange. A fine head, white cheeks and throat are set off by a great black dagger-like bill. His feet are sealing-wax red, and extraordinary because two of the toes are fused into one as far as the second joint. The female looks almost the same but can usually be distinguished by the lower mandible of her bill which is orange.

For colour the common kingfisher can stand comparison with many tropical birds, not that it isn't a tropical bird itself. A glance at the world distribution of the species *Alcedo atthis* shows that about half of them live, literally, between the tropics of Capricorn and Cancer, in Africa, India and south-east Asia. Further south the bird's range extends into South Africa; to the north it ranges from north-west Africa and Europe eastwards across Asia to Japan. But the tropical populations of the common kingfisher, with blue instead of rufous ear-coverts, are believed by ornithologists to be the more primitive type. So the bird appears to have evolved in the tropics and spread later to temperate zones.

Fishing behaviour and diet

When hungry, the common kingfisher characteristically chooses a vantage point, usually a branch overhanging the water, and there it lies in wait for a likely meal to swim into view. When a fish obliges the kingfisher stiffens, tightening its feathers to its body, and casts itself headlong into the water like an arrow. There is a 'plop' and, if it's lucky, it grabs the fish crosswise in the bill, turns itself over from the head down position and, with the aid of the wings, lifts itself out of the water to return to its perch – all within a fraction of a second. If the fish is large or lively – or both – it is beaten into impotence on the bough before being swallowed head first.

The aggressive posture of the kingfisher

Favourite execution blocks often glisten with scales. Where no suitable perches are available, the bird will hover after the manner of a kestrel with body almost vertical, before plunging in the usual way.

The common kingfisher's choice of food depends, among other things, on season, habitat and locality. In India a pair fed their young mainly on frogs; P.O. Swanberg found that minnows were the exclusive diet of broods in Sweden. In Britain the only comparative analysis that has been done puts minnows top of the list, then sticklebacks, gudgeon and trout. But other classes of animal also seem to be important in the kingfisher's gastronomy: among the insects, water boatmen, mayflies, dragonflies, water beetles and others; among the crustaceans, crayfish and freshwater shrimps; and in other classes, tadpoles, earthworms and leeches. All these creatures are, of course, freshwater ones. As soon as a kingfisher moves to estuarine water, or to the seashore, then a very different food spectrum emerges, including shrimps, prawns and small rock fish.

Just how much food a wild kingfisher needs, no one seems to know. But Oskar Heinroth, who kept them in captivity, found that a grown bird required an average of 20 grams of fish a day, plus a number of meal-worms or kitchen cockroaches.

Territoriality

Each pair of common kingfishers defends its own stretch of river. Robert Brown, an inveterate kingfisher watcher who has found over a hundred nests by Scottish rivers in his time, describes an incident involving two cock kingfishers that illustrates how territorial the kingfisher is: 'The cocks were perched on some roots overhanging deep water. From their upright attitudes and the way they faced each other at a distance of a few feet, they resembled a couple of well-drilled soldiers. Now and again one would fly at the

other, attempting to knock his opponent off his perch, and if one
turned his back for a moment the other immediately repeated the
act. Finally they got a good grip of each other's bill, pulling and
tugging as gannets do, and collapsed in a heap into the water.
Retaining their grip, they splashed about in the water for about a
minute before breaking loose.' 'Ducking' fights of this kind have
been seen by a number of observers and are said to be much more
frequent when there is a high number of pairs per mile of river.
Aggressive behaviour can be experimentally released by placing a
stuffed kingfisher on a perch near a known nest.

Nesting cycle

Perhaps the earliest positive sign that kingfishers have breeding in
mind is when one finds them starting to excavate a nest hole,
though in fact this behaviour can precede egg-laying by several
weeks. The work of excavation is shared by the sexes. They hurl
themselves time and again against the chosen spot in the river
bank, trying to get the hole started. It is tiring work until they can
get a proper foothold. Once there is a rim to perch on, tunnelling
proceeds apace. The spade-work is done with the bill, and the feet
send out a shower of earth such as one sees when a terrier is digging
out a rabbit. The point selected is usually above water level, by
between three and six feet, and the distance from the entrance to
the back of the chamber is normally between eighteen inches and
three feet. The type of soil determines the length of the tunnel, and
the sapping may take three to seven days.

Accounts of kingfisher courtship displays are varied and difficult
to match up. Fast circling or figure-of-eight flights by the male are
described; also a slow, wavering butterfly-flight accompanied by
song. Various bowing and bobbing postures have been seen, but
the sexes are not easy to distinguish and no confident interpreta-
tions of behaviour noted have been offered. But on one charming

*An adult kingfisher with
a bullhead for its young*

piece of behaviour many observers agree: the fish-presentation ceremony. Having never been photographed before, it was beautifully filmed by Ron Eastman one lucky April day in 1958.

The commentary to the *Look* film on the kingfisher annotates the event as follows: 'A strange call is heard. The hen is ready for mating, but first, ceremonial must be observed: the "courtship feeding" ritual. On hearing the call, the cock has caught a fish and he holds it head outwards, ready for presentation.' The feeding of food items by a male bird to a female is known for many different kinds of bird at this stage in the reproductive cycle. It was for long thought simply to be a pair-bonding formality, the actual food having symbolic value. But since the film was completed the behaviour has been re-interpreted by the bird people. The fish is now believed also to be important additional food to assist with the production of the eggs. Any number up to seven have to be produced in as many days. The commentary continues: 'The following day the first egg is laid; it is a delicate pink in colour and about half an inch long. Outside, the mating ceremonial is being performed again. The birds mate each day, and four days later the clutch is complete.' The actual copulation was also filmed, also for the first time to the best of our knowledge and belief.

Breeding season

Kingfisher eggs may be laid as early as the last week of March or as late as the last week of August. Many, perhaps most pairs lay two clutches in a season, and some at least go on to attempt three families. The eggs take rather less than three weeks to hatch, and the young take rather more than three weeks to fledge. Incubation duties are shared between the sexes, but usually the female sits at night.

Similarly, the brooding and feeding of the nestlings are shared. 'How kingfishers feed their young, in nature, has never been seen before,' my commentary confidently asserted. 'This privileged view of the birds' family life shows that the fish are not torn up and fed to the young in pieces as some ornithologists had supposed; they're fed whole, even though the fish may be almost as long as the chick.' Only after the film had been shown at the International Ornithological Congress in Oxford in 1966 did we learn of the work of a Bulgarian ornithologist, Tanu Mitchev, who, on the banks of the Danube, had himself in 1963 opened up a kingfisher's nest to photograph the very same happening, and it is his excellent nest photographs that appear here.

The size and number of fish or other prey items brought to the brood by the parents will vary with many different factors. The most systematic work on the problem is again that of Swanberg. His birds caught only minnows. When the young were five days old the fishes brought were 2·5–3 centimetres long; by the time the offspring were seventeen days old the adults were selecting

Young kingfishers grow up —

*4 days old: still blind,
rudimentary feathers in lines
on back and belly*

*8 days old: eyes beginning to open,
as feathers grow
linear arrangement is obscured.
Adult female delivers fish
in head-out position*

*12 days old: eyes fully opened,
a few feathers on crown and flanks
beginning to splay out,
overall 'hedgehog' appearance*

*15 days old: all feathers open,
but the birds are not
as brightly coloured as adults*

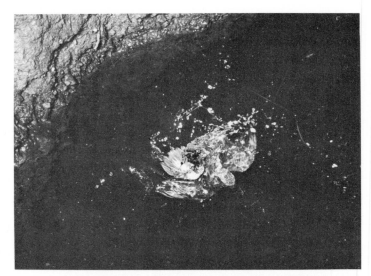

*Kingfisher bathing:
Moment of entry*

*Almost fully immersed,
tail fanned and erected
ready for re-emergence*

minnows 7–8 centimetres long. The total amount of food for the entire nest period of one brood was estimated to be more than a thousand minnows.

Gaining independence

By the time they leave the nest, the young weigh rather more than their parents. This is probably an adaptation to help them over the extremely difficult first few days out of the nest. Jacques Delamain saw a young kingfisher attempting to fish within two hours of leaving home, even though parent kingfishers do feed newly-flown young for a few days. The basic feeding technique of the young ones is instinctive, but practice is needed to perfect it, and the first

*After lifting vertically
from the water
from a quarter-of-a-second dive,
the bird's flight turns
to a horizontal course*

After the bath

few days on their own are an extremely testing time. It is likely that many die, and this contention is supported by the finding of a high proportion of dead ringed birds in August, September and October, most of which are likely to have been born that year. This must be attributable mainly to inexperience. Starvation due to lack of fishing efficiency, and drowning are the two most likely causes.

During the sixty years since bird-ringing began in Britain, about 3,000 kingfishers have been marked with the little numbered metal identity bracelets round their legs. Of these rings, only ninety-seven have subsequently been returned to the organisers. This is a rather small sample but it allows some tentative conclusions. One of the primary purposes of ringing is to discover

Winter and autumn recoveries of kingfishers ringed in Czechoslovakia in spring and summer. Note migration towards coasts of Adriatic, Mediterranean and Atlantic

where birds go to. The ninety-seven recoveries indicate mainly a post breeding-season dispersal of both adults and young. The distances involved, however, are not great, and no British-ringed kingfisher has ever been found abroad. Two-thirds of the birds travelled less than five miles, and only one exceeded a hundred. The directions involved in the more distant recoveries reveal no distinctly preferred direction – if anything, they are in a northerly direction! In Czechoslovakia the kingfisher definitely migrates up to 900 miles, and certainly seeks out coastal areas. Movements as much as 500 miles have already been made by the middle of August.

Causes of death after the first year

If birds of the year survive the difficult post-fledging period, the second major hurdle is the cold weather of midwinter, which has to be faced of course by adults as well as birds of the year. Of this icy hazard more later.

Other less general causes reported by the twenty-four people who have found dead (ringed) kingfishers and who have reported the causes of death include birds being killed by a passing train (two instances), flying into roadside wires or vehicles (nine instances), flying into a window (four), getting tangled in netting (one), and 'drowned in a jar of tiddlers on river bank' (one). Perhaps even more curious than the last is the case of a bird trapped in Co. Durham by the gummy secretion of a chestnut bud which adhered very tightly to the breast feathers of the bird. Fortunately, this particular individual was released by its finder to fish another day.

One of the commonest causes of death reported by finders of ringed birds is 'killed by cat' (seven instances). Predation by cats is important. Ron and Rose Eastman certainly thought the cat a kingfisher enemy on the Test. There is one recent description of how a kingfisher was caught by a cat. A bird that regularly fished a mill stream in Berkshire was using a perch over the water, in the usual way, from which to plunge. The distance horizontally from the point below the perch to the place on the bank from which the cat leapt was five feet. Just as the bird dropped from its perch, the cat sprang, caught it and swam to the bank with it in its mouth. Fortunately for the kingfisher, the cat's owner retrieved the bird and released it apparently unharmed.

It is theoretically possible that some wild British mammals take kingfishers, though it hardly seems likely that they do so on any scale. Predatory birds seem a much more likely threat. But of the half-dozen diurnal birds of prey that might be expected to, only one – the sparrowhawk – has ever been known to do so. This is at first sight rather surprising, for the kingfisher is a small and rather conspicuously coloured bird. But to help overcome these two disadvantages, the process of evolution has given the kingfisher protection of an extraordinarily sophisticated kind.

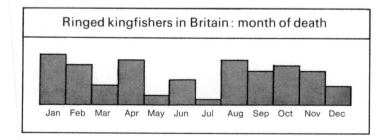

Ringed kingfishers in Britain : month of death

Jan Feb Mar Apr May Jun Jul Aug Sep Oct Nov Dec

Note the three peaks: January–February, due to cold isolating food supply; April, due to stress associated with nesting; August to October, when young birds of the year are inexperienced

Distasteful flesh

In the autumn of 1941, a British zoologist, H. B. Cott, on war service in Egypt, happened to be skinning a kingfisher at Beni Suef in Middle Egypt. He was preparing a specimen for scientific

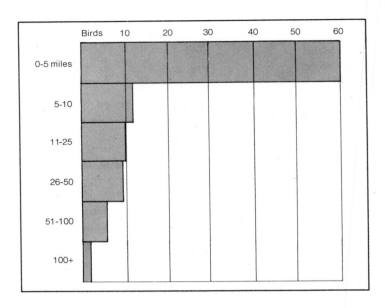

Distances travelled by ringed kingfishers in Britain. The strong stay-at-home tendency is shown by nearly two-thirds of the birds travelling less than five miles

safe-keeping, and threw the fleshy inside of the bird on to the ground. It fell beside the remains of the previous creature he had worked on, a palm dove. Hornets were plentiful in the garden where he was working and soon collected on the meat. But he found that they concentrated almost entirely on the carcass of the dove, neglecting the remains of the kingfisher. Not, one would think, a very significant preference – and yet this simple observation coupled with the imaginative perception of the scientist concerned led to a remarkable discovery. Further research on the meat preferences, not only of insect meat-eaters, but also cats and man himself, showed marked differences in the edibility of different kinds of bird flesh. Furthermore, the more edible the bird was, the more camouflaged its plumage; and, conversely, the more conspicuous its plumage, the more distasteful its flesh. Thus it can be argued that the kingfisher can afford to have its bright colours partly *because* it has evolved unpalatable flesh. But, you might say, of what use is it to be unappetising if your enemy can discover this only after you are dead? The answer is that having distasteful flesh cannot be to the advantage of every individual kingfisher but it can benefit the species as a whole because predators, after trying one, may be deterred from killing others.

Age

Those kingfishers ringed either as nestlings or in their first autumn (young birds of the year have different plumage from adults), and then discovered dead, give us some idea of the likely ages to which British kingfishers live.

The ringing office of the British Trust for Ornithology has

sixty-six such recoveries. Of these birds more than half died before 1 April the following year, that is before they were a year old. Twenty-four died before their second birthday, and seven before they were three years old. Only one lived to more than four years – a bird ringed as a July nestling in 1964, found dead in January 1969. The probable maximum age in the wild would be six or seven years.

These figures, although rather sketchy, do indicate an annual mortality of about 75 per cent, which is high for a non-passerine bird of any kind. The kingfisher is obviously only able to keep alive as a species because it can rear broods of six or seven, not only once but often twice or even three times a year. They raise young successfully to maturity at a rate of about one and a half young per pair per year, a rate which is consistent with their being able to recover their numbers quite quickly when hit by a hard spell – as we know they can do.

Bad winters are killers

The winter of 1962–3 was the coldest since 1740 and only one other winter in British history is known to have been more severe: the 'long frost' of 1684 featured in *Lorna Doone*. Early in 1963 Britain's thousands of week-end bird-watchers kept careful notes on the effects of the prolonged cold spell, and the resulting detailed analyses showed that of the 150 or so resident nesting birds in this country, the one that suffered the worst was the kingfisher. It was hardest hit, of course, because it depends on fresh water being fresh water and not ice. But not only were inland waters frozen solid; the birds that moved coastwards only found that the estuaries were solid too. Even the sea froze in many places.

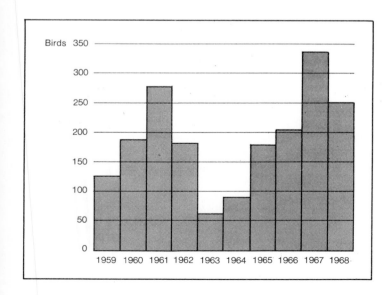

Number of kingfishers ringed in Britain during ten years. Note the sharp decline during 1963 due to hard 1962/3 winter, and steady recovery during next four years

59

Most county reports were of total extermination; no one recorded anything more favourable than 'severe losses', except from three localities. Ron and Rose Eastman found that the Test at Whitchurch in Hampshire remained open and birds were still about, and on the Hampshire/Dorset border ornithologist John Ash found the species surviving in apparently normal numbers. A particularly interesting situation in Cheshire showed that after the ice relaxed its grip and nesting began, kingfishers were still favouring fourteen out of sixteen localities where they had been known to be present in previous breeding seasons. Some fast-flowing rivers here, too, were not frozen, and, further, the effect of the industrial use of river and canal water by power stations and factories may have actually helped the birds. The water thus used is returned to its source unpolluted and at a considerably higher temperature, precluding freezing and considerably stimulating fish.

Unfrozen rivers and industrially warmed water can hardly have been confined to three counties in Britain, and thus the effect on the kingfisher population may have been a little exaggerated. If we examine the numbers of kingfishers marked (as opposed to recovered) by British ringers in each of the ten years 1959–68 they do show a marked drop, but not as severe a one as the general estimates suggested. No one would deny, however, that overall the birds' numbers were most drastically reduced.

Furthermore, we also know that this happens every time there is a severe winter. Going back over the last century: in 1946–7 the bird was 'heavily reduced' in numbers; in 1939–40 it 'suffered severely'; in 1916–17 there were 'considerable decreases in the breeding stock', and in 1890–1 it 'suffered severely'. Emotionally one's response to this recurrent toll is of sadness that so many such beautiful and near-harmless birds should die. But scientifically it must be pointed out that hard weather and kingfishers have been around for tens of thousands of years, and in any case we do know from common observation that the population is resilient and well able to recover its numbers in a few years. Some figures, admittedly not as complete as one would like, are available on the subject. In 1934 a kingfisher count taken along sixty-eight miles of the Thames in the breeding season gave an average of one pair every two miles. That was five years before the severe winter of 1939–40. In 1961, only two breeding seasons, as it happened, before the abnormal weather of 1962–3, another count showed a very similar figure – about one nest every two miles. Now *after* the earlier bad winter, counts made in 1940, 1941 and 1942 showed a pair every thirty miles in 1940, every nine miles in 1941 and every five miles in 1942. Unfortunately, no further years were covered, but a good indication is given of the sort of rate at which the species can recover its numbers. Following the 1963 winter, the members of the Oxford Ornithological Society found that the number had not fallen steeply and one pair was found every twenty miles. By

1966, the fourth subsequent breeding season, the birds' numbers were almost back to normal.

The fact that *fewer* apparently died in the *more* severe winter requires explanation, and this probably lies in the fact that in early 1940 (but not in early 1963) a devastating 'bottle frost' occurred. There was a thick coating of ice over everything following the ice storm of late January. This phenomenon, which is fortunately rare in Britain, even in bad winters, causes birds of a number of species to be frozen to their roosting perches, or else have their plumage sheathed in ice. In either case they would die of starvation. Even in the comparatively mild winter of 1961 a kingfisher was found in Middlesex stuck by frost to a narrow iron pipe over a stream. Still alive, it was hanging by its left leg which was broken in two places. The finder of the bird took it home but it died two days later.

No doubt quite a number of kingfishers die from the direct effects of exposure to frost in severe winters, but the primary cause of death must result from food being locked away beneath the ice. The difficulty is that few alternative foods to freshwater life are available in winter. The famous Norfolk naturalist, Emma Turner, records that in frosty weather a kingfisher was seen taking suet from a bird-table and, more recently, another woman observer has reported from Northamptonshire that after seeing a kingfisher

The mother bird flies to feed her young nested low in the bank of a river

In the nineteenth century kingfishers were often hunted and their rich feathers used for plumes

hovering before some suet hung for tits in her garden, she put out some fish offal. Immediately afterwards it was consumed by two kingfishers. During the 1947 winter a kingfisher in Nottinghamshire was seen feeding on bread scraps. The bird perched on a post from which it dropped down to snatch a piece of bread and return to its perch. It is thus clear that some individuals at least are adaptable.

General status in Britain

The effects of hard winters aside, the general status of the kingfisher in these islands gives no real cause for despair. To deal first with Ireland, a very recent survey using appeals for information in the Press as well as to bird-watchers in the island indicates that 'Ireland can claim to have a good population', with no signs of a decline. In England and Wales there is no evidence to show that the numbers of nesting kingfishers have appreciably altered during this century, except possibly that river pollution might have affected the bird in a few places in central and southern England. Of its status in Scotland John Parslow writes that 'it had locally become common in the Lowlands by the 1930s [and] has recently decreased very markedly. In several counties the main decline appears to have occurred with the hard winter of 1947, while in those in which the species did not then become extinct it has since gradually decreased almost to vanishing point.' Except for three, there appear to be no Scottish counties where the bird now certainly breeds annually. River pollution has been blamed for this Scottish decrease.

Kingfisher and man

During the nineteenth century the kingfisher was deliberately killed by man for a variety of reasons. Being so brightly coloured, it was much in demand as a stuffed ornament for Victorian drawing-rooms. But the overall number shot for this purpose can hardly have been very great. A few were taken, ironically enough, to provide feathers for fishing flies, but again, not many would have been involved. Before the Wild Birds Protection Acts put a stop to the evil practice, many more kingfishers must have been netted for the plume trade, the feathers being used to decorate ladies' hats. As recently as August 1911 no less than twenty-two kingfishers were caught on a short stretch of the Ching Brook at Woodford in Essex. The specially-designed kingfisher net used really consisted of two nets, one with a very large mesh and the other with a very fine one. Hunters would stretch these nets under bridges and then drive birds up- or down-stream towards them. When the bird flew into one, it pulled the small-mesh net through one of the 'holes' of the large-mesh net, neatly trapping itself. The net was still in use in Belgium where a big demand existed, at least until 1964, for stuffed set-up specimens.

Fisherman v. fisherbird

It was because the fisherman and the river-keeper saw the kingfisher as a competitor that large numbers of these birds were
destroyed. In particular, their attraction to trout hatcheries was
their downfall and it remains somewhat of a problem to this day.
The Hampshire Test is the most famous trout river in Britain and
for fifty years William Lunn was a river-keeper on one of the
stretches. One year he put about seven thousand fry into a small
nursery. He covered it with small-mesh wire and until June all was
well. Then fish began to disappear. One morning at first light Lunn
found, under the wire, sixteen kingfishers! They had found a hole
under the netting and Lunn claimed that they consumed three
thousand of his fry. This may be an exaggeration but there can be
no doubt that on rare occasions kingfisher predation can be costly.
But no economic loss could surely justify the use of cruel pole-
traps, and yet they were widely used. In the first decade of the
century as many as fifteen kingfishers were caught in a week or two
as they alighted on one particular stump placed in one hatchery
specially for the purpose. Even more inhumane was the blocking-
up of nesting holes leaving the young to die slowly of starvation.

In Denmark just after the Second World War a questionnaire
was sent to about sixty owners of commercial fish-rearing establish-
ments, enquiring about the occurrence and behaviour of the kingfisher. The birds turned up most commonly in autumn and winter,
usually only one at a time. To a question asking whether the visitors
did any noteworthy damage to fish fry, eight out of ten replied
negatively; the remainder, however, maintained that the bird did
considerable damage. There seems to be no doubt that at certain
hatcheries kingfishers do take numbers of fish fry but it can only be
in exceptional cases that economic losses of any significance are
involved. Nylon nets are now employed in Danish Government
research hatcheries to keep out kingfishers and also to deter larger
birds such as terns, but at other hatcheries, although the species is
protected generally by law, individual offenders may be shot, and
doubtless birds are, whether they truly offend or not. In Switzerland there is much the same situation: the bird is legally protected
but, for example, eighty kingfishers are known to have been killed
at one hatchery in a single recent autumn. It was claimed that it was
not only the fish they ate that gave offence, but those they wounded
became diseased, causing much wider mortality. To make matters
even worse, it has also been suggested that the pollution of Swiss
rivers make the concentrations of birds at hatcheries even greater.

A direct threat to potential nesting sites is the 'improvement' of
banks by river authorities. A German bird protectionist recently
described methods for artificial nesting sites both by preparing
holes in the walls of 'canalised' waterways, and by providing
mounds of suitable soil. The kingfisher does show a certain, if

rather limited, flexibility in its choice of home, and might thus be helped in this way. As long ago as 1916 a pair of kingfishers successfully reared three young from an artificial concrete tunnel in a dam near Newport in Monmouthshire. In Hampshire thirty years later C.R. Tubbs found a nest in a post on the Farlington Marshes near Portsmouth. The post was about seven feet high and the nest was in a split which the birds had enlarged. This curious site had been in use for some years. In Holland the rationalisation of small streams has reduced the country's nesting kingfishers to a tenth of their number some years before. The Eastmans' experiences in successfully persuading kingfishers to adopt a man-made bank are encouraging in this respect.

Poisoned water

By the deliberate discharge into existing rivers and streams of his domestic and industrial waste man greatly alters the composition of the plant and animal communities of fresh water. Almost invariably the result is an impoverishment of the wildlife spectrum. The kingfisher is believed to have suffered from pollution not only in Switzerland, but also in Denmark, the Netherlands, Luxemburg, and possibly southern Scotland and central and southern England.

Besides domestic and industrial pollution there is the spectre of the persistent toxic pesticides. Measurable concentrations are to be found in all environments in Britain, and in almost all wild birds and their eggs. In April 1967 a kingfisher picked up dead by professional ornithologist Chris Mead was found on post-mortem analysis to have 'exceptionally high' concentrations of DDT, DDE, Dieldrin and PCB in its liver. Since no one knows what is a fatal dose of toxic chemicals to a kingfisher, it is impossible to say with absolute certainty that chemicals killed this bird. It does, however, seem highly likely.

The kingfisher is a bird at the top of a food chain involving many organisms in the wet places of our countryside. Water is easily contaminated. The large predatory fishes like the pike occupy the same position at the top of the food pyramid, and are threatened in the same way. Luckily for man, the flesh of these fishes is less likely to be contaminated than the guts he throws away. The kingfisher is less fortunate; he swallows his prey whole and collects another full dose each time.

There is no evidence that in some areas the levels of some but not all pesticides are decreasing currently as a result of a voluntary ban on their use but it is vital from the bird-protectionist viewpoint that restrictions should continue in force until sufficient time has elapsed for firm conclusions to be reached.

The 'secret splendour of the brooks' may be less secret as ornithologists discover more and more, but he is no less splendid, and for that reason alone the kingfisher, and the web of river life of which he is part, are worth the conscious effort of conservation.

Courtship feeding

Copulating

Three newly-fledged young kingfishers

Fishing under water

The Greater Horseshoe Bat   *John Hooper*

Bats, active only at twilight or in darkness and retiring at other times to secluded and often inaccessible hiding places, are not easy to observe and this account must necessarily pose almost as many questions as it answers. In the past, the nocturnal and seemingly secretive habits of bats earned them a rather sinister reputation and mention of 'bats' immediately conjured up thoughts of superstition, witchcraft and vampires. Even today superstition dies hard. The phrase 'as blind as a bat' is still often heard, despite its lack of foundation, and the old wives' tale of bats becoming inextricably tangled in women's hair is widely believed in spite of convincing demonstrations to the contrary. To most people, probably, a bat is just a bat, and even to naturalists it sometimes comes as a surprise to learn just how many species there are. As Desmond Morris once neatly pointed out in a television programme, 'About a quarter of the 4,237 living species of mammals have developed the ability to fly. One species is man and the other 981 are all bats.' Bats, however, can fly naturally, like birds, and the flight of a bat is true flight, in which height can be gained and lost at will – and thus differs from the action of the so-called 'flying mammals', for example the flying squirrels, which merely make long gliding jumps during which height is lost.

Bats belong to the order Chiroptera, meaning 'wing-handed', and it is easy to see how this name arose. Each wing – a flexible membrane of skin – is attached to the side of the body and also the leg but in effect is an extension of the arm and, in particular, of the hand. The arm bones, especially the forearm, are elongated, giving strength to the inner half of the wing, but it is the finger bones, enormously long and spanning the wing from front to rear, which impart rigidity and control to the main 'aerodynamic surface'. In contrast to these great fingers, the thumb is almost rudimentary – a short claw, protruding forward and mainly used as an aid to crawling. The wings, at the rear, extend down the legs as far as the ankles, and between each leg and the slender tail there is a further flap of skin.

The greater horseshoe bat

This chapter is confined to just one species – the greater horseshoe bat *(Rhinolophus ferrumequinum)* – but this is not to say that this bat is either typical or the most common. Its choice stems from

*Greater horseshoe bat,
showing how the tail membrane
folds over to fill the gap
between the folded wings*

the fact that, due to its habit of wintering in caves, it is relatively easy to find and has thus been easier to study than other species. It is not found on the American continent, but is widely distributed for example over Japan, many parts of Asia, and south and central Europe. In the British Isles it is absent from Scotland, Ireland, north Wales and the northern counties of England, but is found in most southern counties of England and is particularly common in the southwest and in south Wales. This may well be a reflection of the large number of suitable underground haunts in the west country, since this species is essentially a 'cave-dweller'. There are many natural limestone caves in south Wales, Somerset (notably in the Mendip Hills) and Devon, and other underground haunts include old stone quarries, as for example near Swanage, in Dorset, or the extensive Bath stone workings in Somerset, or the similar tunnels near Beer, in Devon. To these may be added disused stone and ochre workings in Gloucestershire, old mine tunnels in the Forest of Dean, and literally hundreds more disused mine workings and test adits further west, particularly in Devon and Cornwall. In all such tunnels, both greater and lesser horseshoe bats (as well as other species) may be found.

To study the private life of a greater horseshoe bat one must visit a cave, and since my wife and I have been studying bats in Devon caves since 1948, let us take, as a typical haunt, one of the complex natural caverns at Buckfastleigh, in the valley of the River Dart. In fact, almost any tunnel, whether natural or man-made, as long as it is not too wet and not too draughty, is likely to suit a bat – it meets the desired needs for seclusion, darkness and acceptable conditions of temperature and humidity. It does not have to be a long cave, and we may equally well find bats almost within sight of daylight, or several hundred yards from the entrance. In the latter event, it will probably be necessary to squeeze through tight rifts and crawl along low tunnels – close-fitting to the human frame, but no obstacle to a bat. In any such cave, from mid-October onwards, there is a good chance of finding sleeping bats, at least during the daylight hours. If the bat is a greater horseshoe, it is easy to spot. Unlike Natterer's bats, which normally tuck themselves deeply into narrow crevices, the horseshoe bats hang quite openly from walls or roof of a passage. From a distance they look like fat, dark-brown pears dangling from the bare rock – and they may be found hanging alone, or in little groups of half a dozen or so, or sometimes almost by the hundred in clusters so tightly packed that individual bodies are indistinguishable.

When sleeping, the greater horseshoe bat hangs with wings tightly wrapped around the body, the forearms side by side down the middle of the back and the wrists touching just beneath the head so that the folded wings enshroud ears as well as face. From below, all that can be seen of its head will be a glimpse of pink nose and a few whiskers. Above, the tail flap is folded over the back to cover the gap between the wings, and the only exposed members are the feet, each with five delicate claws, curved over to obtain a surprisingly firm grip on minute ridges in the rock. If we stop to take a close look, the bat will react by bending its knees, and these bend in the opposite direction to those of man. The legs look almost too fragile to support its weight, and yet a sleeping greater horseshoe can hang quite securely by only one leg, with the other tucked in beneath its wing. They also hang by one leg while they conduct their toilet, using the claws of the other as a comb. The action is similar to that of a cat, the bat moistening its claws in its mouth and then combing the fur with a rapid scratching movement. They clean themselves very thoroughly and also use the tongue to lick their wings, meanwhile going through a variety of contortions as they pivot on a leg whose joints allow a remarkable degree of rotation.

The greater horseshoe bat, when hanging at rest, measures about $3\frac{1}{2}$ inches from feet to nose, whereas the lesser horseshoe bat, which sleeps in similar fashion, is roughly $2\frac{1}{2}$ inches. These are the only British bats which sleep with their wings wrapped round them. With the horseshoe bats the grotesque nasal membrane presents an unmistakable feature. This is a large pink disc or 'nose-leaf' covering most of the face and shaped like a horseshoe at the bottom – hence the name. The two nostrils lie in a depression at the centre of the disc and immediately above these a wedge-shaped spike, known as the *sella*, protrudes forward. At the top, right across the centre of the 'forehead', the nose-leaf ends in an upward spear of skin called the *lancet*. The eyes are set close in to the nose-leaf and the rather dainty lips below it are not obvious when closed. They look less dainty when open, and conceal a large mouth whose jaws

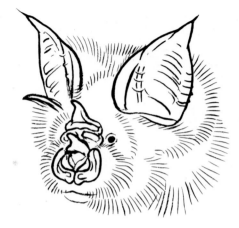

Drawing showing the nasal membrane from which the horseshoe bat derives its name

Greater horseshoe bat and lesser horseshoe bat

*The sharp teeth
of the greater horseshoe bat*

can open unexpectedly wide – a fact which can be painfully discovered if an angry bat is incautiously handled, since the two rows of sharp teeth can readily puncture human skin. The ears are large and pointed, and the body is thickly covered with fine, almost silken fur, generally tawny-brown in appearance, with a slight mauvish tinge. Variation between individuals does occur, so that some bats appear grey, while others are almost ginger in colour. The wings are brown, with a pinkish cast, the surface being faceted with myriads of tiny wrinkles that are very noticeable when the wings are folded at rest. If they are held against the light a network of fine veins and blood-vessels may be seen. The greater horseshoe, one of the largest British bats, has a wing-span of from 12–14 inches.

Autumn behaviour

Until about Christmas the greater horseshoe bats remain quite active. Although spending many hours in sleep, they leave their tunnels each evening to hunt for insects and do not necessarily return to the same haunt, often travelling to other tunnels many miles away. In moving from haunt to haunt, they show no particular consistency of habit. At Buckfastleigh, for example, there are at least fifty caves or mine-workings within a radius of five miles and these various tunnels support what may loosely be described as a 'colony' of about 150 greater horseshoe bats. These do not behave as an integrated colony in the sense that one talks of a colony of bees, and the movements of the individual bats, seemingly random, produce shifting, temporary groups which remain constant neither in size nor composition. An individual might thus be found on one occasion in a group of six, a week later in another cave, by itself or with an entirely different group, and later on somewhere else again, in a big cluster of fifty or more. The reason why such large clusters – which might have fifty or sixty bats in less than a square foot – are formed is not too clear. When a bat sleeps, its temperature drops to that of the surrounding air, so that all that clustering could do would be to slow down the cooling-off process for those in the middle. In Devon we have found these tightly packed clusters most commonly during periods of cold weather, but this may not be the whole story, and autumn clusters, for example, could be associated with mating activities. Certainly these groupings contain bats of both sexes and the earlier belief that they segregated into separate groups according to sex is not correct. There is, however, no intermingling of sleeping horseshoe bats with bats of other species.

Copulation takes place in the autumn, usually about October or November. This is quite promiscuous, with no evidence of pairing off. Birth does not take place until the following July, and during the winter months the male sperm is trapped and retained, within a firm, jelly-like plug, at the upper end of the female's vagina, which thus seals off the uterus. Ovulation, followed by fertilisation by this stored sperm, does not take place until April, when the bats become active again with the onset of warmer weather. The reason for this 'delayed implantation', as biologists call it, is uncertain, but it ensures that the baby is born at a season when food is plentiful, and in time to reach maturity before winter starts.

Survival in winter

The problem which faces the horseshoe bat every winter is that of survival – of keeping alive throughout a long period of semi-starvation when insect food is scarce. To do this, it has to rely on such energy reserves as it can hold in the form of stored fat. This means that the bat has to build up an adequate reserve at the start of the winter, to 'top up' by hunting for insects when conditions permit, and, above all, to economise on energy consumption by spending long periods in a state of torpidity, the so-called hiber-nation. For the greater horseshoe bat such 'hibernation' is by no means continuous. It appears to wake every few days, and this is probably necessary – quite apart from any hunting activity – to allow the bat to take in moisture and avoid desiccation. Weighing experiments which we carried out in Devon for four winters in succession showed that they continue to hunt, with profit, at least until mid-December, when their average weight reaches a peak value, but after this the weight falls off rapidly, the decline con-tinuing until about April. During this decline such bats decrease in weight by almost one-third, a typical drop being from 24 grams in December to less than 17 grams in mid-April. Bats certainly leave the caves to hunt in the early months of the year, but the balance between fat used up in flying, and fresh food caught is precarious and could well go the wrong way if insects were hard to

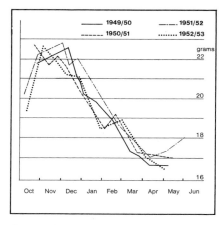

Seasonal variations in weight

Cluster of greater horseshoe bats, each with its identification ring

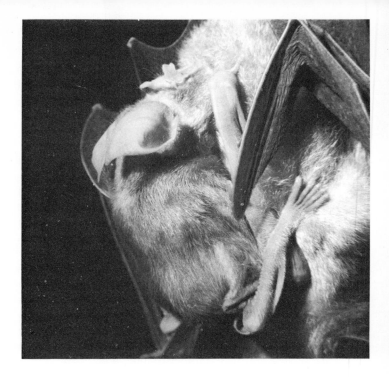

A baby bat clinging with feet, wings and mouth to the underside of its mother

find. It follows therefore that any unnecessary flights resulting, say, from thoughtless human disturbance could have serious effects and could mean death from starvation later in the winter. Anyone who does visit a cave in winter and see sleeping bats should remember this and do nothing to disturb them. Handling, noise, lights – any of these can be enough to cause the bat to wake up and fly off.

This highlights one of the difficulties in studying such bats. They react, even when seemingly fast asleep, to human presence, and if this reaction develops to full wakefulness, the ultrasonic 'shouts' (see p. 74) which the bat will start to emit prior to flight will wake up other bats nearby, and these in turn will do the same thing and soon the entire cluster will be disturbed. In other words, any attempt to keep track of the activities of a bat colony in a cave, by making frequent visits, would probably defeat its own purpose by inducing artificial activity which would not otherwise have occurred.

Summer activity

In April or May, with the return of warmer weather, the bats become more active and move out to roosts in barns and house roofs. For the females that were mated during the previous autumn, such summer activity is followed by ovulation and fertilisation by the stored sperm that they have been carrying during the intervening months. They give birth to their young in late June/early July, but the date varies from year to year and is, for example, delayed if emergence from the caves is held back by a spell of cold weather in the spring. Just before the young are born, the females gather together in some convenient roof to form a large 'nursing colony'. We know that some males, probably young ones, are tolerated in such colonies, but it is difficult to take an accurate census, partly because the bats will not stay still to be counted, dispersing in a cloud of wings immediately their privacy is invaded by a human being, and – more important – because such disturbance would probably lead to desertion of the haunt and possible abandonment of babies already born.

The baby bat, born while the mother hangs from the rafters, has the characteristic horseshoe nose, disproportionately large in comparison with the undeveloped head, and is a helpless little creature, initially blind, with soft, pinkish-white wings. At birth, it is about the size of a human thumb and is born with fur on. It clings to its mother with claws, feet and mouth and maintains a sufficiently firm grip to allow itself to be carried while the mother is in flight. Horseshoe bats give birth to only a single baby each year, twins being exceptionally rare. The mothers have two extra nipples in the groin; these are 'dummy teats' which yield no milk and serve merely to give the baby a firm anchorage point. For feeding, it has to transfer its attention to the lactating nipples on its mother's chest. The young bat develops rapidly and its fur becomes long and sleek and noticeably darker than that of its mother. This shows up particularly well when the latter is in flight, with the large, grey lump of her baby attached to her underside. The baby, gripping its mother's false nipples with its teeth, is of course carried through the air upside down and backwards! Within a week or so its weight will be fully half that of its mother, and in consequence a burdensome load to be carried around during hunting manoeuvres. For this reason, presumably, the females, when they leave their

Young horseshoe bat being carried on the underside of its parent in flight

Two young greater horseshoe bats sleeping peacefully, awaiting the return of their mothers

Captive greater horseshoe bat tackling an outsize cockroach

roof to hunt each evening, normally 'park' their offspring on the rafters and fly out unencumbered. This provides the human observer with an opportunity for a visit to the 'nursery' without any fear of upsetting the adults. Such a nursery is a sight well worth seeing – possibly twenty or thirty juveniles, ranging in age from tiny things barely a day old to comparatively mature individuals of two or three weeks, the latter scrabbling furiously on the rafters but not yet able to fly. Some will hang quietly asleep, while others break out at intervals in bursts of high-pitched squeaks – a characteristic 'chittering' sound which can be equally noisy when the adults are present. The means whereby the mother persuades her offspring to let go of her, turn itself the other way up and get a grip on the roof, is not clear but the manoeuvre is carried out very expeditiously, as also is the reverse process when she returns, about an hour later.

After three or four weeks the juveniles can fly on their own and quickly learn the art of catching insects for themselves, so that weaning is complete by mid-August. The diet of the greater horseshoe bat is not known in full detail, but includes cockchafers, black dung beetles and similar 'large' prey, as well as moths and spiders. These bats often carry their insect catch (at least the larger items) to definite 'feeding posts', such as a cave entrance, where they settle while they feed. The carrying of insects in the mouth does not interfere with their ability to guide their flight using ultrasonic signals, since the latter are emitted through the nostrils. Beneath their feeding posts, it is possible to find uneaten portions of their catch, discarded wings and legs for example, and these give a useful clue to the bats' diet.

Movements

In the autumn the horseshoe bats resume their usage of caves, and the juveniles, now fully grown, are no longer easy to distinguish from the adults. This movement, from caves to house roofs and back again, each year, is easy to understand, but other movements are not so readily explained. Roger Ransome, studying greater horseshoe bats in Somerset and Gloucestershire, has given much thought to the problem of why bats move around between caves and has pointed out that, in winter at least, the presence or absence of bats in a particular haunt may be correlated with temperature (which can vary markedly between caves, and even between different parts of the same cave). He suggests that the temperature of the haunt controls the frequency of waking, as dictated by the need to hunt, and that the bat chooses its sleeping place on the basis of the temperature there, relating this in some way to the insect density outside (also affected by temperature) when it last hunted. This is a reasonable explanation, but seems likely to apply essentially to 'local' rather than long-distance movements. It is difficult, for example, to visualise a bat setting off with the intention of

The greater horseshoe bat

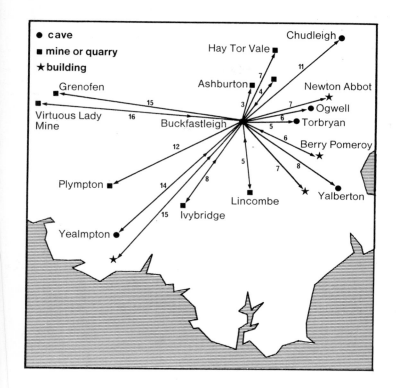

*Typical flights of
greater horseshoe bats from a colony
at Buckfastleigh in Devon.
Numerals give straight-line mileages
and the arrows indicate
the direction of the flights*

travelling to 'a better 'ole' some fifteen miles distant! And yet they
obviously have considerable skill at finding remote tunnels. How,
as often happens, does a greater horseshoe bat locate an isolated
mine adit in open fields, miles from any other tunnel? How is it that
bats are able to find and occupy, within a matter of days of its
discovery by potholers, a new cave entrance opened up at a place
where previously there was only earth and solid rock? Why should
a greater horseshoe bat fly, during a period of a few weeks, from
some underground stone quarries in Devon to a cowshed in Dorset
forty miles away? And why, a few months later, should it make the
return journey? This movement of forty miles is the longest flight
so far recorded for a bat in Britain, but obviously we do not know
how many stages the journey took, nor how direct it was. Movements between haunts five to fifteen miles apart are comparatively
common for this species and many of them, surprisingly, take
place in midwinter. In Devon, where we have built up a list of over
150 haunts used by bats, no very clear pattern of movement has
emerged apart from a suggestion that greater horseshoes born in
one of the major colonies, for example, in the caves at Buckfastleigh, tend, after a few years, to move out to and settle in some more
distant tunnel, possibly ten miles away. We certainly have many
records of bats which, having made such a move, are then found
year after year in their new haunt and are not seen again (at least,

Infant grey seal awaiting the return of its dam from the sea   73

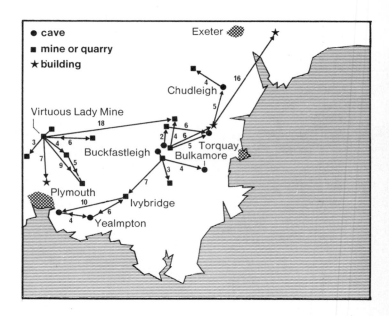

*Typical cross-country movements
of greater horseshoe bats in Devon*

not on the occasion of our visits) in the region of their birthplace. In some cases the new haunt is an isolated tunnel with only two or three such inhabitants, but occasionally a bat moves from its original colony to join, and settle with, a major colony in another area. Such interchange of members takes place from time to time between the otherwise separate groups of greater horseshoe bats inhabiting the caves at Buckfastleigh and at Chudleigh, eleven miles apart. Clearly much remains to be learned on the subject of bat movements.

Our knowledge of such bat peregrinations is obtained through the use of rings, following the technique employed for birds. For bats, the rings used are narrow bands of aluminium, shaped like the letter 'C'. The two ends of the 'C' are gently clamped round the forearm of the bat so that they meet, but do not pierce, the wing membrane. It is thus not shaken off by wing movement, and is too light to affect the flight of the bat. It bears a number and an address so that findings can be reported. In Britain, there is now a National Bat Banding Scheme under the aegis of the Mammal Society, and the rings used bear the simple address 'LOND. ZOO'. Bat banding is not a subject to be undertaken lightly or on a short-term basis and needs to be strictly controlled to ensure that properly designed rings are used which will not harm the bats and that the activities of separate groups of workers do not overlap.

Ultrasonics

The ability of bats to orientate themselves by means of high-frequency sounds is now well known and the greater horseshoe bat, as is demonstrated by the ease with which it skims through constricted cave passages in complete darkness, possesses this ability to a fine degree. This is not to say that bats do not also use their eyes, but when there is no light they have to rely on hearing alone. As a bat flies, it emits a succession of short 'pulses' of sound, so high in frequency that they are far above the range detectable by the human ear. Detection of echoes reflected back from obstacles in its course enables the bat to judge (by means not fully understood) the direction and range of such obstacles, so that it is able to avoid flying into them. The same system is used to locate and intercept flying insects for food. For some bats each pulse of 'ultrasound' is very short indeed and sweeps down from a high to a lower frequency (typically from about 80,000 down to 30,000 cycles per second) in only about 2 milliseconds (1/500th of a second). The ultrasounds of the greater horseshoe bat follow a different pattern. Firstly, each pulse is relatively long, usually at least 50 milliseconds, and secondly it remains essentially at a constant, particularly high frequency during this period – about 85,000 cycles per second.

When flying, the greater horseshoe emits these constant-frequency sounds, rather like trumpet blasts, at a rate of about ten a second, and the trumpet analogy is not unreasonable since the sounds emerge from the nostrils, not the mouth, and the horn–like aperture of the nose-leaf helps to concentrate these sounds into a forward-pointing beam. This scans the darkness ahead of the bat (in the same way that we might use a torch beam) and, as high-speed cinephotography has shown, the emission of ultrasounds is accompanied by synchronised swivelling movements of the large ears. These bats can judge their position relative to obstacles with great precision, and when they land on a passage roof, for example, they fly straight to it and flip over at the very last moment so that their feet touch and get a grip on the rock and they come to rest in a hanging position.

Much has been learned by 'bat-men' during recent years concerning the ultrasounds of bats following the development of transistorised 'ultrasonic receivers' (powered by batteries) which are small enough and portable enough to be taken into caves and other bat haunts. These receivers have a special microphone sensitive to high frequencies, and can be tuned to pick up the frequencies emitted most strongly by the bat. The instrument 'translates' these down to lower frequencies which can be heard by the human ear, the result coming out of a loudspeaker as a click or a 'chirrup'. For the greater horseshoe bat the loudspeaker emits a series of shrill barks, rather like the yapping of some dogs. It is fascinating to visit a cave when a cluster of greater horseshoe bats is waking up in readiness to hunt. When the 'bat detector' is switched on, the silence of the cave is broken by a tremendous chorus of barks and chirrups from the loudspeaker and, listening to such a confused babel of sound, it is difficult to understand how

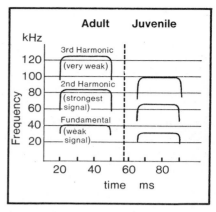

Typical frequency-time diagram for ultrasonic signal emitted by a greater horseshoe bat, showing how the pattern for the juvenile is similar to that of adult but at a lower frequency

75

*Problem for a bat man:
how to persuade a young bat
not to climb out of the scale
pan up to the beam!*

the individual bats are able to distinguish their own echoes amidst all the rest of the noise. Such ultrasounds are intended solely to help the bat orientate itself, and should not be confused with the fairly expressive vocabulary of audible squeaks which it can also utter, as for example when it is angry. In the nursing colonies, also, the adults seem to become very talkative at times, squeaking almost as much as their offspring. The baby bats, incidentally, develop the power to emit ultrasounds at an early age, and certainly well before they are able to fly.

Health and longevity

Bats are not, as sometimes believed, excessively verminous – their meticulous toilet activities see to this – but they do occasionally harbour a blood-sucking ecto-parasite, such as a tick. These gain access to sleeping bats from the cave walls, attaching themselves, with head buried in the bat's skin, often at a place, for example the back of the neck, where they are difficult to dislodge. They subsequently drop off, having gorged themselves with blood.

Since the female only has one young each year, and will not have her first offspring until she is at least two and more usually three years old, a long life is essential if the species is to be perpetuated. Just how long that life can be is now emerging from the various banding experiments in progress. In Devon, where bat banding has been going on longest (having started in 1948), the oldest greater horseshoe bat so far found is one which (from the date of its initial ringing) was at least $19\frac{1}{4}$ years old. As the work continues even older bats may be found, but enough records of 16-year-old greater horseshoes have already been obtained to establish that this latter age, at least, is not uncommon for the species.

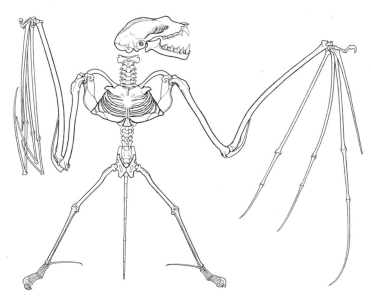

Skeleton of the greater horseshoe bat

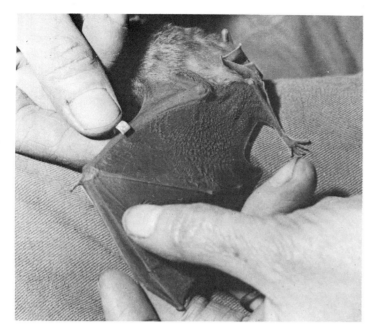

Ringing a bat

The risks of death from starvation have already been emphasised, but apart from this, the greater horseshoe bat seems to lead
a fairly healthy life. Death must often occur when the bat is hanging
asleep, and occasionally a skeleton is found hanging from the roof,
its claws still gripping the rock although the body they once
supported has long decayed away. Bats appear to have few natural
enemies, apart perhaps from owls, but nevertheless recent observations in some areas have suggested that their population may be
declining. If this is true, and the decline is real and not part of some
long-term cyclic change, then the agent responsible is probably
man. Many tunnels used by bats have been bulldozed in, or
quarried away in land development operations, and bats, as insect-
eaters, are of course particularly prone to poisoning, through
cumulative build-up of traces of organo-chloride and other sprays
carried by the insects they catch. Many bats are needlessly exterminated when householders complain of colonies in their attics,
vicars drive them from their churches, and collectors for museums
or medical research have been known to deplete whole colonies
regardless of long-term consequences. This chapter therefore
closes with a plea for tolerance, not only for the greater horseshoe
bat, but for bats in general. A bat may not be 'man's best friend',
but at least it is harmless and does much good work in keeping down
insect populations, so it is not unreasonable to counsel a policy of
'Live and let live' – and for the greater horseshoe bat 'let live' means
'Do not disturb' when it is found asleep in winter.

The Atlantic Grey Seal   *J. Morton Boyd*

The first step in understanding seals is to realise that they are built to the same pattern as a terrestrial animal – a mammal. All the organ systems, body form and function are *primarily* intended for running, not swimming. At some distant point in evolutionary time nature had second thoughts about some of the early mammals. Some, having developed far enough along the road to terrestrial life to acquire the basic form, returned to the sea to become the stock of marine mammals – the seals, sea-lions, walruses, sea-cows and whales. The basic processes of locomotion, sensory reception, temperature control, respiration, digestion and reproduction have remained unchanged; the morphology and physiology has, however, been strongly adapted for life in the sea and for breeding on land.

Take the shape: they are perfectly streamlined in the water. Their bodies, moulded as it were by the water pressure, appear to give no propelling thrust as they glide in effortless dive, turn and somersault. The nostrils are superb watertight valves and the eyes, having no tear ducts, are continuously wet even when out of the sea. Heat loss is controlled by a two-inch layer of blubber with a meagre blood supply to the outer skin. The teeth are sharp, capable of seizing and tearing but not of chewing, and the gut is that of a carnivore. Water intake is in food and this means a great deal of salt, the level of which is controlled by a kidney capable of excreting a highly salty urine. The penis possesses a bone and is to some extent prehensile in copulation. The milk has 60 per cent fat compared with 3·5 per cent in domestic cows. Oxygen is stored not only in the blood but also in the muscle cells, enabling the seal to remain underwater for long periods.

Some marine mammals have travelled further than others in their return journey to the sea. For example, whales conduct their whole life cycle without contacting land at any time; if, accidentally, they do so, they will die. Some seals, like the common or harbour seal which inhabits the British coasts, need very little contact with land, giving birth to their calves on tidal banks and nursing them in the sea. The grey or Atlantic seal *(Halichoerus grypus)*, as we shall see later, has much more dependence on land. It comes ashore for several weeks to give birth to calves, which are nursed and deserted by the dam on land, and to copulate above high-water mark.

78

The circus 'seals' which balance a ball on their noses are usually sea-lions which are 'eared'. The grey seal is a true or 'earless' seal which is unable to reflect its hind flippers forward, sit up and beg, or shuffle around quickly on all fours. The sea-lions and fur seals are athletic, with strong, mobile limbs without claws; the true seals, on the other hand, are clumsy with weak, prehensile limbs possessing claws. In the grey seal the fore-flipper grips the surf-swept rocks, but forward motion comes not from the limbs but from the massive body musculature, in cumbersome, looping thrusts from the pelvic girdle.

Identifying the grey seal

The grey seal, like all of its kind, is a beautiful, sensitive creature with large, soft, intelligent eyes. It can be distinguished from the common seal by its blunt, rather massive, Roman nose; the common seal has a pointed snout and looks rather like a dog in the water. The grey seal is also larger when adult and is characteristically blotched, while the common seal is spotted. They are, however, very difficult to distinguish in the field mainly because of the wide range of colour and marking in both species and because juvenile grey seals are the same size as adult common seals. No coastal habitat is exclusive to one and not the other, but the common seal is not in fact common (except in some parts of Shetland) on exposed rocky coasts, where the grey seal is very much at home in the stormy inlets. Assemblies of seals in the Wash, on the Abertay Sands, Beauly Firth and Firth of Lorne are likely to be common seals; those on the Farne Islands, Pentland Skerries, Fair Isle, St Kilda and Skerryvore are almost certain to be grey seals.

Part of a winter-spring assembly of 350 grey seals, Pembrokeshire

Grey seal bull, North Rona

The grey seal bull is generally not grey in colour; the popular name is derived from the colour of the cows where grey predominates. Bulls range from dark umber to pale buff, with many olive-brown or dark iron-grey and few with extensive blotching. Often they blend perfectly with their beds of seaweed. A full-grown bull will be eight or nine feet overall and will probably weigh more than seven hundredweight. In late summer, when in first-class condition, the old bulls have great rolls of blubber and skin around the neck. These quickly disappear during the enforced fast on the breeding grounds when there is no time for feeding. The continuous defence of territories precludes going to sea.

In the sea the bull is distinguished by the much more massive muzzle and broader head than the cow, but on land the difference between the sexes is more striking. The full-grown cow is about seven feet long and probably weighs about four or five hundredweight depending on the state of pregnancy. She is a beautifully dressed lady with a steel-grey head, back and flippers; the underside from chin to groin is pale yellow ochre splashed with browns and blacks and sometimes with chestnut shading on the throat. The dominant bull is a formidable creature as he hauls himself – a quivering mass of fat and muscle – out of the sea to claim his breeding territory. The young cow, coming ashore, say, to deliver her first calf, is a radiant, slim figure in a dappled, shining coat.

Calving

The calves are born between September and December, though there are records of births in almost every month of the year. The delivery is like the pop of a champagne cork with the calf

J. Morton Boyd with day-old grey seal weighing about 32 lb., North Rona

Grey seal cow suckling, North Rona. The calves are fed at about two-hourly intervals for the first few days, then at longer intervals

Grey seals off North Rona, looking like great sorrowful dogs

landing well clear of the dam. The newly-born calf is stained yellow by the birth fluids, is thin and weighs about 32 lb. Within a week the youngster, clad in its cream-coloured infant coat, already shows signs of putting on weight and of being able to defend itself against intruding gulls; it will even snarl and try to escape from a human intruder. Suckling usually lasts about seventeen days and the calf now weighs about 85 lb., having had an average daily weight increase of about 3·5 lb.; some have been known to put on more than 5 lb. in one day. During the nursing period the calf has developed from a thin, feeble creature to a plump, tight bag of energy, possessing immense strength for its size.

While the calf grows it also loses its white coat. Even after a week some calves begin to show darkening on the muzzle and on the extremities of the flippers. After three weeks the calf is in full moult and more often than not is deserted by its mother when resplendent in its first sea-going livery and while lying in a bed of its cast infant coat. They are then known as 'moulters'.

Female moulters have a lustrous blue-grey coat; male moulters have an equally fine dark-grey and occasionally a jet-black one. It is these velvety pelts which are much sought by the sealers of the Northern and Western Isles of Scotland. After the mother departs the moulter begins to wander and may spend between two and three weeks moving through the breeding assembly, spending long periods asleep and splashing in tidal pools. Ultimately it enters the sea and departs for distant waters, but there is no sign of its obtaining any upbringing in the sea where it probably acts innately. The moulters quickly disperse over hundreds of miles of sea after leaving the nursery; within a few weeks of leaving North Rona, some forty-five miles north-west of Cape Wrath, they have been reported as far afield as east Iceland (480 miles), southern Norway (390 miles) and Northern Ireland (300 miles).

A month-old grey seal calf lies near its cast infant coat, North Rona

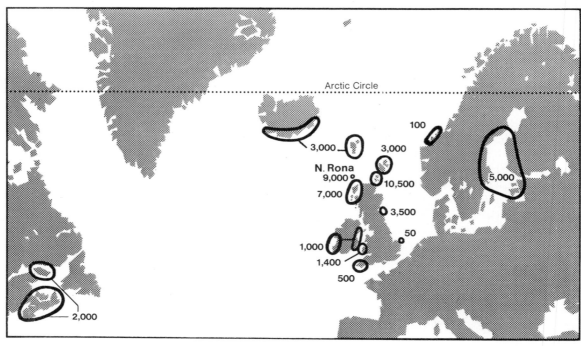

Arctic Circle

3,000

100

3,000

N. Rona
9,000

10,500

7,000

5,000

3,500

50

1,000

1,400

500

2,000

The distribution and approximate size of known breeding colonies of grey seals in the North Atlantic

How many grey seals are there?

In 1963 the world population of grey seals was thought to be 46,000, of which 36,000 frequented the British Isles. It breeds in small numbers in Norway, Faroes and Iceland and other populations, much smaller than that of the north-east Atlantic, occur in the Gulf of Bothnia and eastern Canada and Newfoundland. The main breeding stations are the Farne Islands, Orkney, North Rona and the Outer Hebrides (Gasker, Shillay, Coppay and Haskeir). North Rona (320 acres) is the largest single assembly in the world – about 9,000 seals of all ages – which almost certainly became established after the island was deserted by man in 1844. A minor assembly breeds on St Kilda where none existed when the islands were inhabited before 1930. The withdrawal of man as a permanent inhabitant from the remote islands of the north-west fringe of Britain, the decline in the use of seal products during the second half of last and the first half of this century, and the Grey Seal Protection Acts of 1914 and 1932, have resulted in an increase in numbers and a need for conservation in relationship to fisheries.

Seals as migrants

It has been possible to follow the movements of young seals by branding and tagging. Such marking programmes have been in

The Population of Grey Seals

	Number	Percentage of Total
Orkney (counts)	10,500	23
Shetland (partly counts)	3,000	7
North Rona (counts)	9,000	19
North-west Scotland (partly counts) ...	7,000	15
Total, Scotland	29,500	64
Farnes (counts)	3,500	8
Pembrokeshire (counts)	1,400	3
Cornwall and Scilly (rough estimate) ...	500	1
Ireland (rough estimate)	1,000	2
Total, England, Wales and Ireland ...	6,400	14
Iceland and Faroes (rough estimate) ...	3,000	7
Norway (rough estimate)	100	—
Total, North-east Atlantic	39,000	85
Baltic (rough estimate)	5,000	11
North-west Atlantic (mainly Canadian Maritime Provinces) (partly counts) ...	2,000	4
Total, all areas	46,000	100

progress over the last ten years on the Farne Islands and North Rona. The recoveries from these and others in Orkney, Pembrokeshire and the Hebrides show that the population of grey seals breeding in the British Isles ranges very widely from Iceland to the Dutch coast, and from Ireland to the Norwegian coast, and that there is overlap in the ranges of seals from the main breeding centres. Unfortunately, few of the tags survive more than a year and it is for this reason that branding has been adopted as the most satisfactory method of providing long-term identification. By observations of branded seals it should be possible to trace the movements of adults to and from the breeding islands in autumn

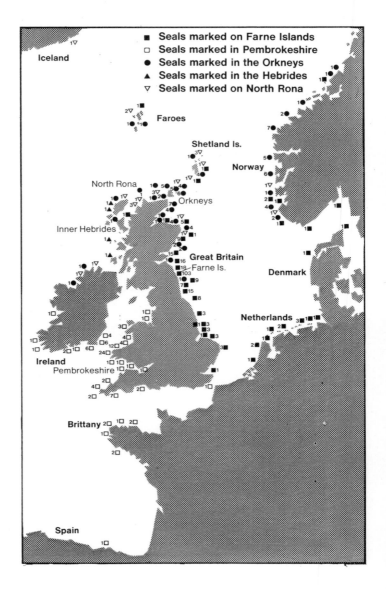

The total number of returns of
seals tagged around
the British coasts

and early-winter, where those which damage fishing-nets came from and whether or not they return to breed on the island of their birth. All these questions are of vital importance to the conservation of the grey seal.

The breeding season of the grey seal commences in late August and early September at North Rona. The bulls are first to arrive and haul out *en masse* on the off-lying skerries and tidal shelves opposite the main access routes to the breeding grounds on the two low promontories of Fianuis and Sceapull. Throughout September the large, dominant bulls come ashore and take up territories until in some areas there is a firm patchwork of occupied, vigorously defended ground. A few bulls prefer to be on their own, taking up detached positions, and others ascend a steep grassy hill to stake their claims on the ridge of the island, some 250 feet above the sea. It is to the dense patchwork, however, that the cows come in greatest numbers and though the detached bulls may have a more peaceful time, they have less sexual activity. The bull does not herd his cows; he simply claims those which choose to calve within the geographical limits of his territory and the closer he is to the mainstream of cows coming ashore, the more he is likely to acquire on his land.

While the bulls are engaged in defence and challenge, the cows come ashore in small numbers in September, but in a great rush in October, to deliver their calves. The territories of the dominant bulls fill with gravid cows and the assembly spreads gradually landward until even the detached bulls at the back have a few cows with them. In the packs a master bull may have as many as twenty cows on his land and with the appearance of the calves in October the ground becomes congested and muddy. The peak of calving at North Rona (it is different for different assemblies throughout Britain) is about 12 October, when some eighty calves are born daily. The total number born annually at North Rona is over 2,000, and in Great Britain as a whole probably about 9,000.

Grey seals mating, North Rona

A fully moulted calf
showing the beautiful 'blue' coat.
Recently left by its mother,
it has not yet reached the sea

Infant mortality

About 20 per cent of the calves at North Rona die before they reach the sea. This is a high mortality when compared with other assemblies where the figure can be less than 5 per cent. Mortality is low where the territories of the bulls are arranged linearly along the shore as they are in most of the Orkney assemblies and in the Treshnish Isles, Inner Hebrides. With such an arrangement the animals pass directly from sea to territory without interaction between bulls and without narrow channelling of heavy traffic. Mortality is high in the patchwork arrangement, such as occurs at North Rona, Farne Islands and Gasker (Harris), with constant transgressions of adults in the presence of defenceless calves. The situation is made more dangerous for many calves born within or near the main access gullies. Strenuous activity by adults causes calves to be run over or badly bitten. Bulls have no regard for calves and will lumber over very young ones causing grievous injury or death; cows in the tight packs bicker jealously and calves are bitten by strange dams. Paradoxically, detached cows have been seen to foster hungry, deserted calves.

Cows are enigmatic in their motherhood. Some will desert the calf on a first appearance of man and will not return, while others will stay to defend the calf against all comers. Some take little heed of danger to their calf, allowing it to wander and be negligently injured or killed, while others will go to great pains to save their offspring, particularly when the calf falls into the surf. Some cows, probably young ones, lose their calf at birth by withdrawing a few yards from the newly-born, wriggling infant. Instantly, great black-backed gulls are on the scene tearing, tugging and pecking at the afterbirth and calf; only the swift return of the dam will save her calf and the numbers of maimed gulls flapping pathetically around the seal grounds are testimony to such swift action.

The maternal instinct in the same cow may vary within a few days. When the calf is young, the urge to mother the offspring is likely to be strong. At the end of the nursing when she is coming into oestrus, the maternal instincts may be substantially replaced by those of mating. Quite soon after mating the cow disappears.

Territorial bulls

Strange as it may seem, it is not the big territory bulls of September and early October which are responsible for the insemination of the greatest number of cows. The largest number of cows on North Rona come to oestrus in late October, following the peak of calving on 12 October. By that time most of the original territory holders have been replaced by challengers, probably younger bulls fresh from the sea.

Fights between bulls are common but rarely result in serious injury and very rarely in death. Fights are often precipitated by human interference pushing the animals together when they would otherwise judiciously avoid each other. Old bulls bear the scars of many seasons of challenge and defence on the breeding grounds and their ages are often roughly judged by the extent of the scarring. Fights often result in the contestants bleeding from deep bitten gashes on muzzle and shoulder. Both animals stand face to face with waving heads held high and mouths open, snarling viciously. The weight is taken on one flipper, the other is used for slashing the adversary. There is lunge, thrust and snap with occasional grip and shake. The bout may last only a few seconds but often for many minutes, after which the vanquished moves

A light-coloured youngster, also fully moulted. At four weeks old it weighs a little under 100 lb.

away quickly and the victor, having successfully seen him off the premises, may sometimes do a victory roll.

Cows are mated in the territories of bulls soon after lactation is complete, and before the uterus has healed following the parturition of the calf only three weeks previously. The cow ovulates, the ovum is fertilised but instead of the embryo developing immediately it lies dormant in the uterus for about five months, after which it is implanted in the uterus and develops in a gestation period of about seven months. This delayed implantation has an obvious advantage for the seal; it completes the whole reproductive cycle in one highly concentrated spasm of activity and obviates the need for separate calving and mating season with the concomitant problems of energy loss. Mating in autumn and calving in spring would not put the calves at such a great risk of death in some assemblies, but the high calf mortality may in fact be a blessing in disguise; it may be an important means of natural control of numbers at a healthy level.

By the end of November the seal grounds of North Rona are once again almost deserted. The throngs of seals have left acres of mud and the tattered remains of dead calves. It is not known where they go after leaving the breeding islands though the recovery of moulters already mentioned indicates wide dispersal to feeding stations. Lighthousemen and fishermen find the local grey seal haunts becoming repopulated in spring and there is probably a great deal of wandering and exploration, particularly among juvenile animals. For example, many more juveniles than adults are found at fishing nets. The social groupings both on the breeding grounds and when widely dispersed are unknown. In an animal so highly developed as the grey seal, however, it would be surprising if the companies on the nurseries, in the moulting assemblies in spring, and on the haul-out rocks at the far-flung feeding grounds were not bound by a strong social order.

In the past twenty years the grey seal has been brought more and more to the attention of the public as a threat to coastal salmon fisheries and also to white-fish stocks, through parasitic infection. Out of this has come the Suspension of Close Season Order, renewed annually, by which the Minister of Agriculture, Fisheries and Food and the Secretary of State for Scotland are able to issue permits for the culling of grey seals during the breeding season. There has never before been such widespread concern about its numerical status, impact upon human economy and enchantment as a beautiful animal. The grey seal is an outstanding part of our heritage of wildlife in Britain and it is gratifying to know that legislation is now before Parliament to overhaul the law governing its conservation in the light of improved knowledge.

The Great Crested Grebe   *K. E. L. Simmons*

The great crested grebe *(Podiceps cristatus)* – graceful ornament of so many of our lakes, reservoirs and gravel-pits – gets its name from its size (being the biggest of the five Eurasian grebes) and from the dark, elongated, double crest on its crown which it wears in all plumages after the downy stage. In its basic 'eclipse' plumage of the later months of the year, the grebe is simply grey-brown above and pure white below. This typical counter-shading is characteristic of many birds that swim underwater and probably helps to camouflage them when hunting. For much of the year, from mid-winter onwards until early autumn, the great crested grebe wears its special 'display' plumage. In addition to the ever-present crest, the bird grows a beautiful, velvety 'tippet' on each side of the head; this is deep chestnut and black in colour and frames its white face. The flanks also become chestnut in contrast to the duller grey-brown of the upper parts. Both crest and tippets are highly erectile and are used in the various courtship ceremonies for which this species is famous (see pp. 94, 95 and 97).

The body feathers of the grebe are very dense and waterproof, especially those of the breast and belly which once provided the satiny 'grebe fur' used by ladies of fashion during the nineteenth century in much the same way as mammal pelts are still used for capes, muffs and hats. Indeed, commercial persecution in the British Isles was so severe that by the mid-1800s the species' numbers had crashed to below a hundred individuals and the grebe was in danger of extinction here, a perilous situation from which it was rescued by protective legislation. Since then it has increased dramatically until today there are about 5,000 individual adults in England, Scotland and Wales. During recent decades this increase has been assisted by the availability of new, man-made waters in the form of reservoirs and gravel-pits. But now another danger threatens, even more insidious than the old – that of poisoning by the persistent, toxic chemicals used in agriculture. These seep into waters and accumulate progressively in organisms all along the food-chain. Fortunately, so far, the grebe appears to be the least affected of all our fish-eating waterbirds.

Underwater fisherman

The great crested grebe is above all the quintessential waterbird. It lives on and under the water for most of its life, only occasionally

First phase of Head-shaking Ceremony: the birds meet, face and call, waggling their heads rapidly

flying and seldom coming voluntarily to dry land. Its body is designed to make it a highly efficient, torpedo-like, underwater diver and pursuer of fish. The bill is long and pointed, the neck long and thin. The wings are proportionally small and curved so as to fit closely against the contours of the back where they disappear among the overlapping flank feathers. The tail is a rudimentary tuft. Finally, the large and powerful feet are placed right at the rear of the body; with lobed and partially webbed toes, they screw the bird through the water at great speed. However, the grebe swims much more slowly on the surface and if there is any urgency it prefers to travel from point to point under the water. So great is its tie with water that it can afford, in late summer and early autumn, to shed all the wing feathers simultaneously and risk being flightless for the four or more weeks it takes for the new ones to grow. In advance of this vulnerable stage, many birds leave the smaller breeding waters and gather to moult on much larger lakes (such as Chew Valley Lake in Somerset) or on the sea where they are much safer from predators.

Every day of its life, the great crested grebe alternates between spells of fishing and 'loafing', the proportion of time spent at each depending mainly on how readily available the local food is. On waters where there are plenty of the bigger coarse fish it favours (such as roach), the grebe can obtain a substantial meal easily and spends relatively little time hunting. But on other waters where it has to feed largely on small 'tiddlers', this can occupy well over half its time. A typical spell of fishing consists of a series of dives underwater with a pause on the surface between each dive. The mean duration of its hunting-dive is less than half a minute on many shallower waters but may exceed this if the water is deeper – say well over ten feet – but still works out at well below a minute.

Underwater, the grebe enters a very private world of its own where it is hidden from close observation. But it would seem that there its method is to pursue shoals of fish at high speed and usually to eat smaller-sized prey without surfacing. If, however, a fish of over about three inches in length is caught, then the bird rises to eat it above water. It can swallow fish of up to seven inches fairly easily but may have to abandon the occasional one that is longer or too thick for even its distensible jaw to manage. Sometimes, however, quite small fish of two inches or less are brought to the surface and the grebe spends a disproportionately long time in dealing with them – flicking them in the bill and working them in and out of the mouth rather like a man eating a hot potato. These fish are sticklebacks whose dorsal spines stand erect and rigid until death.

As well as diving conventionally for food, the grebe fishes in another way which, though not uncommon, is less well known. In shallow water, or over submerged vegetation, it swims on the surface with only its bill and eyes under at first, peering for food just below the water. When it sights something it then submerges its head and neck and finally up-ends or plunges after it, causing much turbulence. Great crested grebes are usually solitary hunters but at certain times, for example during the last summer gatherings of moulting birds, many individuals may congregate over dense shoals

Second phase of Head-shaking Ceremony :
the birds silently waggle and sway their heads

91

of fish. At favoured wintering areas, too, scores of grebes may collect together when loafing.

Grebe toilet

After a fishing spell the grebe often has a bathe. The normal ablution is quite brief with the bird simply alternating a few times between ducking its head under the water and rubbing its bill and face along the flanks. In a more thorough bathe, it also thrashes the water with half-open wings and paddles round in an upright position with the wings trailing down below water. Occasionally – perhaps only once a day or even less – it has a really good wetting. Ruffling up all its feathers, it kick-dives repeatedly under the water with a flick of the wings to swim just below the surface before eventually carrying out all the other bathing movements. Whether it has bathed or not, the grebe almost invariably preens its feathers during a loafing spell and usually oils them as well – a vital procedure for so aquatic a bird. It gets oil from the preen-gland at the base of its back both with the bill and by rolling the head over the gland. Then using its head virtually as an oily 'mop' it rubs the oil over much of the rest of the plumage. After a 'dive-bathing' session, special attention is given to oiling the wings, not only with the aid of bill and head but also by repeatedly twitching the wings on the back so that the primary tips themselves contact the gland.

While preening, the grebe will actually eat any of its own body feathers that become detached, rather than discarding them! The feathers collect in the stomach where they disintegrate to form a felt-like ball. The exact function of this peculiar habit, which is found only in the grebe family, is much debated but it is agreed that the feathers play some role in digestion – either by acting as a 'plug' to retain fish bones in the stomach until they are absorbed, or as a basis for ejectable pellets.

Pairing up

Great crested grebes start to pair up in midwinter, hence the early growth of the 'display' plumage. Some pairs start prospecting

Mating Ceremony :
Invitation-display on weed platform

Mating Ceremony:
Rearing-display

for nest-sites and setting up territory as early as December or January, depending on the severity of winter. Disputes over mates – or in defence of the mate or territory – may be intense and lead to quite serious fights in which the combatants grapple breast to breast and try to force each other under the water. Attacks may also be made over the water or from below it. However, as with the majority of birds, much of the fighting is harmless and ritualised, consisting largely of threat – chiefly 'barking' and 'growling' calls and the *Forward-display.* In the latter, the bird stretches its neck out near the surface of the water with the tippets flared out, often with its back feathers ruffled or, less frequently, with the wings partly 'swanned' over the back showing their white markings.

The great crested grebe may be regarded as an opportunist nester. In the British Isles it has a protracted laying season lasting until August or even September. Although many pairs produce eggs from May onwards, the birds on some waters nest earlier than this – in March and April or even occasionally in February. So grebe eggs can be found in eight months of the year. Much depends on the presence of suitable cover for the nest though each local population seems also to have a 'tradition' of whether it breeds as early in the year as it can, or waits (even to July or August) until the seasonal vegetation is denser. The pressure exerted by the local predators, chiefly carrion crows and other egg-thieves, is probably a major factor, as is disturbance by man. Thus, although many great crested grebes pair up and establish territory early, it may be many weeks (or even months) before conditions become suitable for nesting. Hence there is often a long 'engagement' period during which they may face intense competition from rivals for their mates and nest-sites. It is during this time – from the initial pairing until functional mating occurs – that the grebes carry out their ritual courtship ceremonies in which both sexes take equal part, either playing identical roles or different but interchangeable ones. There is nothing private about the courtship of the great crested grebe for the four main ceremonies are carried out in full view on open water for all to see. They also occur at night, especially by moonlight when the white parts of the birds' plumage show up conspicuously.

Courtship

Either sex can take the initiative in courtship, both during early pairing and the later engagement stage, the bird often drawing attention to itself by vocal *Advertising* (p. 96). The most common of the courting rituals is the *Head-shaking Ceremony* (pp. 90, 91) which occurs about five times more often than all the other ceremonies put together. It acts mainly as a 'greeting' and, in its full form, has three distinct phases. In the first, male and female face each other closely, both rapidly waggling the head with erect neck but bill 'hanging'. The tippets are spread fully into a flower-like, circular ruff and the crest bristles forward like a two-pronged horn. A 'ticking' call is uttered continuously. Then the birds abruptly stop calling, raise their heads, partly depress the tippets and alternately waggle the head more freely and sway it slowly from side to side. In turn, this second phase merges into a third in which the birds now also *Habit-preen* – formally dipping the head backwards for a moment to flick up some scapular feathers with the bill.

Head-shaking may sometimes be preceded by an elaborate introductory ritual, the *Discovery Ceremony* (p. 95), especially after male and female have been wholly separated beforehand. The returning bird swims towards its mate only just under the water (the *Ripple-approach*), periodically carrying out quick 'sightings' with only the head showing. It finally emerges vertically out of the water, close to and beyond the other bird, in the weird *Ghostly-penguin Display*, turns its back on it and then, rotating to face it, subsides and starts *Head-shaking*. Meanwhile, the first bird has assumed the equally strange *Cat-display* with head low and tippets expanded and the wings extended in a V on each side, their upper surfaces tilted forward to show the white markings. Finally, it rotates to face the mate as the latter, after its last 'sighting', swims under it to emerge on the far side. The 'cat' bird then folds away its wings and joins with its mate in the silent, second phase of the *Head-shaking Ceremony* that follows.

Forward-display:
the bird on the left is threatening
the bird on the right

94

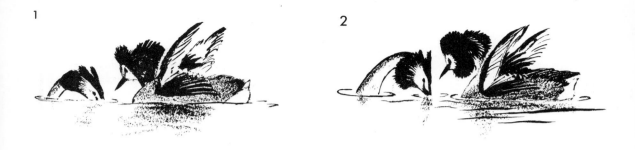

1

2

3

4

Discovery Ceremony:
four stages in which
the bird on the left emerges from the water
in the Ghostly-penguin Display,
while its mate assumes the Cat-display

Discovery Ceremony:
after rotating in the water, the bird
on the left faces its mate again before
subsiding and Head-shaking with it

Head-shaking often merely peters out with the two birds, for example, just drifting apart or preening. However, there are two further ceremonies which provide a ritual sequel to it. The less frequent of these is the *Retreat Ceremony* in which one bird, during the second phase of *Head-shaking*, suddenly patters away over the water past its mate before subsiding several yards away in the *Cat-display*. The stationary bird, meanwhile, sometimes also does a *Cat-display* too and both rotate to face one another. Afterwards, they either drift apart or link-up to *Head-shake* again, occasionally then performing a second *Retreat Ceremony* – often with their roles reversed.

The more common of the ritual sequels to *Head-shaking* is the complex *Weed Ceremony* (p. 97). Following prolonged *Habit-preening*, first one and then the other bird formally turns away from the mate and *Sails-away* over the water, giving the 'twanging' call. Slowly swimming with tippets spread and raked forward, crest depressed laterally, they get farther and farther apart before submerging in a special *Deliberate-dive* and searching for weed underwater. After surfacing, they swim quickly straight towards one another carrying the weed, at the last moment rising breast to breast vertically, almost completely out of the water, feet treading vigorously in the celebrated *Penguin-dance*. In this position, they rapidly point their bills in strict synchronisation from side to side in a continuous *Weed-swinging* movement before, sooner or later, subsiding and shaking away the weed to initiate a final bout of *Head-shaking*. Once thought to be rare, the *Penguin-dance* is in fact fairly common though only about one in every two *Weed Ceremonies* ends with it, mainly because of the failure of one or both birds to bring up weed after doing the *Deliberate-dive*.

Grebe language

Apart from the 'ticking' associated with *Head-shaking* and the 'twanging' with *Sailing-away*, the great crested grebe does not call much during its courtship rituals – unlike that very vocal species, the little grebe. However, the larger bird does call conspicuously when *Advertising* – though this behaviour is shown by solitary birds only, either when seeking a mate or (if paired) when separated from the partner. Thus, it is often a prelude to the *Discovery Ceremony*. When *Advertising*, the grebe floats or swims slowly with neck erect uttering a far-carrying 'croaking' (or 'trumpeting') call, the calling ending when the second bird is located. When together but not actually courting, the male and female keep in contact by 'twanging' and 'clucking' to one another. When further apart, they may 'bark' or 'growl'. Occasionally, during bouts of normal fishing, the male may pass a fish to the female – but such *Fish-presentation* has rarely been seen and requires much further study.

Head-shaking ceremony

Incubating bird threatening intruder

a

b

Weed Ceremony:
after the Head-shaking Ceremony
(a) the birds formally turn away
from one another and
(b) Sail-away over the water,
calling quietly. After diving for weed
the birds (c) swim quickly
towards one another,
and (d), treading water vigorously,
they rise in the Penguin-dance

c

d

Mating Ceremony : copulation

Mating Ceremony

After an initial period of intense courtship, the birds visit potential nest-sites, build mating platforms there, solicit and copulate – sometimes weeks or months before eggs are laid. Thus the *Mating Ceremony,* though quite distinct from the courtship proper, probably plays a somewhat similar role during the potentially long engagement period. It also helps the birds to select sites in readiness for eventual breeding as well as leading to eventual fertilisation, of course. There are two soliciting displays performed freely by either sex. The first is *Inviting* (p. 92), in which the bird lies prone on the platform with neck extended giving the 'twanging' call. The other is *Rearing* (p. 93), in which it stands up suddenly, arching the head and neck down grotesquely, and quivers the closed wings rapidly two or three times to show the white markings (*Wing-flashing*). Though it is usually the male that mounts, reversed mating also occurs not infrequently. Loud calls are given during the *Mating Ceremony* – a loud, peevish 'mooing' before mounting and a harsh 'rattle' during it.

Nests

As we have seen, predation seems to be the most important factor determining the dispersion of nests. Where the fringing vegetation is uniform and narrow, the nests of neighbouring pairs are well spaced out so that they are less easily found. But where there is extensive dense cover (such as large reed beds) or other safe sites (such as groups of flooded willow bushes), then the local birds may well nest closer together in a loose colony – especially if sites are otherwise scarce. Both sexes build the floating nest and take equal shares in incubating the eggs. The normal clutch consists of three or four eggs (but there may be only two or as many as five or even six). As these are laid at 48-hour intervals and incubation usually starts with the first egg, the young hatch at similar intervals so that the youngest chick may be a week or so behind the eldest and correspondingly smaller.

Such asynchronous hatching is unusual for a species with precocial young and is almost certainly linked (as are many of the grebe's breeding adaptations) with the possibility of food shortage while the chicks are still dependent on their parents. Such a situation arises, of course, from the habit of opportunistic nesting which gives the species no clear-cut, peak laying season for hatching to coincide with dependable supplies of food (as is the case with the majority of British birds).

Young grebes

The young great crested grebe is covered with down at birth – white below and conspicuously striped above, particularly on the head. On each side of the pied bill are bare patches of facial skin with a third bare area on the crown. Normally these are pale pink but at moments of excitement they flush deep red. During the pro-

An incubating bird

Change-over of brooding duties

The young are brooded on the parent's back

longed hatching phase, the chicks normally remain with the incubating parent at the nest – not under it but high and dry in the 'tent' on its back, under the wings – while the second adult brings food. The nest is abandoned as soon as the last chick has hatched and the family takes to the water, the young continuing to spend their time in the safety of the floating, mobile 'nest' provided by the parent's back for most of the following two weeks. The adults alternate between carrying the brood and providing food for them – the diet being one largely of fish, supplemented at first by insects and throughout by feathers. Indeed, when newly hatched and still subsisting largely on absorbed yolk, the chick is given more feathers than live food. Later, when the young have taken to the water, the parents take turns to guard them though, if the brood is large, they may soon both have to go fishing simultaneously in

Seven-week-old chick being fed fish by parent

order to meet the great demand (estimated at over 20,000 small fish in twelve weeks for a family of four chicks).

The young are full-grown in about seven weeks but are then still flightless. The wings are fully developed in eight or nine weeks and the juvenile can fly in its eleventh week. Although the chicks can dive virtually at birth, they do not start catching fish until the end of the eighth week or during the ninth after which they are semi-dependent for a variable period. Some leave the parents during the eleventh week more or less as soon as they can fly but others remain, often getting most or all of their own food, until the eighteenth week or longer. However, parental feeding may occasionally continue up to the twenty-second week (at least).

The occasional prolonged feeding of the juvenile is just one of a remarkable set of breeding adaptations that ensures the survival of at least some young should there be uncertainty of food supplies before they are entirely self-sufficient. The most striking of such adaptations is the unusual system of often dividing the brood between the parents when this is of two or more chicks. Then male and female each eventually takes over the care of certain young only, and actually refuses to feed the other chicks. Further, within each family sub-group, each parent may have a 'favourite' chick which associates more closely with it than the rest and which gets priority at feeding. It is this chick that tends to hang on with 'its' adult after the others have gained independence.

This, then, is a little of the private life of the great crested grebe – waterbird extraordinary.

The Large White Butterfly *Claude Rivers*

The leisurely flight of the large white butterfly *(Pieris brassicae)* conjures up in the mind a peaceful scene of green grass, leafy trees and lazy summer days. Farmers who have experienced the damage which this insect can cause to cabbage crops greet the first large white – or 'cabbage' butterfly – with a frown, but to nature lovers it is as sure a sign of summer as the sight of the first swallow.

The first butterflies on the wing have passed the winter as chrysalids concealed under fence rails and in the niches on or inside barns and outbuildings. When the temperatures reach 60° or more the butterflies start to form within their chrysalids and they emerge within a week. Later in the summer more white butterflies fly in from the continent to swell their numbers and these fine insects may be seen at any time from May to September.

The best-known British butterfly!

If the large white butterfly is not the commonest British butterfly it is certainly the best-known. It is a fine insect measuring about two and a quarter inches across the wing tips, and the predominating white wings are marked with black on the upper surface and dusty yellow beneath. The sexes are distinct in that the females have two conspicuous black spots in the centre of the forewing in addition to the black tip. Both sexes have black spots on the underside of the forewings and it is possible to confuse the sexes if the butterflies are examined with their wings closed. When the sun is shining the females sit with their wings partially open and the characteristic black spots displayed. The spring butterflies are less heavily marked with black than the summer-bred ones so that, with a little practice, it is easy to recognise those which have over-wintered as pupae.

Large white butterflies are very fond of fields of broad beans or clover because they afford plenty of food and dense cover for concealment, as well as protection during spells of bad weather. Butterflies have a long tongue or proboscis through which they draw up the nectar from the centre of the flowers. The proboscis is carried curled beneath the head like the hairspring of a watch when the butterfly is not feeding, and is uncoiled and starts to probe in response to the smell of food. Butterflies recognise flowers by their colour and they show a preference for certain colours. White

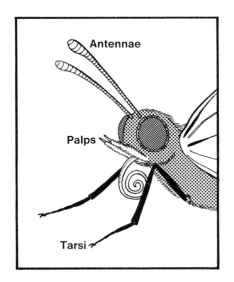

Antennae

Palps

Tarsi

butterflies like yellow flowers and will experimentally settle on and smell pieces of paper or other material coloured yellow. The feeding response is stimulated by the smell of honey which the butterflies detect through their feet, and through their antennae and the palps which shield the proboscis. If you have a captive butterfly you can test this simply by touching the feet or other sensitive parts with a camel-hair brush which has been dipped in a solution of honey or sugar.

The Large White's enemies

Birds are the worst enemies of large white butterflies and the most important of these are sparrows, starlings, flycatchers, blue and great tits, and jackdaws. Ants, spiders and beetles will eat butterflies but they usually catch only the older and weaker individuals.

The active life of the white butterfly is less than a fortnight although it is able to survive for longer than this if a spell of bad weather intervenes. White butterflies take no interest in cabbages during the first few days of their life and they are most often seen in the lanes and fields and are very fond of settling amongst stinging nettles. The virgin female sits on the surface of a leaf in the sunshine with her wings open so that any passing male may recognise her by the black spots on the forewings. The males quarter the field with a characteristic searching flight and will stop and investigate anything which vaguely resembles a white butterfly. A discarded cigarette packet will receive a brief inspection before the butterfly passes on its way. When a female is discovered the male hovers above her for a moment so that he will be recognised by his scent. The female butterfly responds by fluttering her wings for a while and then closes them as the male settles beside her on the

The large – or 'cabbage' – white butterfly

Large white butterflies copulating

leaf. The male clasps the tip of the female abdomen by curving his body forward. As soon as the female is secured the male moves directly behind and the two butterflies sit with closed wings – the wings of the male on the outside.

Mating and egg-laying

Mating usually takes place in dense foliage where the butterflies are not readily seen, as they are very vulnerable at this time. The male flies off if they are disturbed and carries the female with it to a fresh site. Copulation lasts for an hour or two and both butterflies may mate more than once in their lifetime.

White butterflies use colour to help differentiate between various objects. When they are hungry they are attracted to yellow; when a male is searching for a female it looks out for white objects, while a fertilised female seeks out cabbage green. The butterfly's well-developed sense of smell ensures that eggs are only laid on food-plants suitable for the young caterpillars and it is possible to see this sensing taking place. The butterfly flutters briefly over any likely plant, then grips the edge of a leaf with her feet and 'drums' with her forelegs to check that it has the right smell. If she is happy with the situation she settles on the underside with the forelegs gripping the leaf edge. The first egg is laid at once and others follow until 30–100 have been neatly arranged in a batch. After each egg is laid the female carefully feels for this with the tip of her abdomen before placing another next to it. Eggs are usually laid on the underside of cabbage leaves – particularly brussels sprouts, and broccoli.

Female having just laid a batch of eggs

Parent grebe carrying a chick on its back

Adult feeding feather to chick

*Large white butterfly showing
the spot markings*

Except that they are only a millimetre high, the butterfly's eggs resemble corn-cobs

The eggs are bottle-shaped and deep yellow, and have longitudinal ribs and fine transverse ribbing. Except that they are only a millimetre high, they resemble corn on the cob. The female glues them firmly to the leaf as they are laid so that they can withstand wind and rain. The time taken by the eggs to hatch depends upon the temperature but eight days is about the usual period, although many eggs are eaten by predatory mites, ladybird beetles, hover-flies and spiders. When the eggs are a few days old they change to a paler yellow and they darken to brown later still when the larvae are ready to emerge.

Eggs about to hatch

The emergence of the caterpillar

On emergence the larvae measure a little over two millimetres and have black shiny heads with a few white hairs, a smooth greenish body with six rows of tubercles along the back. Caterpillars obtain their air through spiracles on each segment of the body and these are seen as brown spots along each side of these newly-hatched larvae. Before they start to feed on the leaf they spin a silk pad so that they have a secure place on which to live. At first they eat the undersurface of the leaf only, as their jaws are not strong enough to tackle the leaf edge. When feeding they always stretch forward and chew downwards pushing the leaf into their mouths as their jaws work from side to side. The larvae have well-defined segmentation with the three pairs of 'true' legs of the insect poorly developed and a pair of legs to five of the abdominal segments. The head has six simple eyes on each side, and the antennae, so conspicuous in adults, are present but undeveloped. Alongside the jaws the caterpillar has spinnerets for the production of the silk which they use to make a pathway before them wherever they go. This silk-spinning not only ensures that the larvae maintain a foothold on the plant but it helps to keep the colonies together as they follow the trails left by each other. If by any chance it does get

*Newly hatched
large white caterpillars*

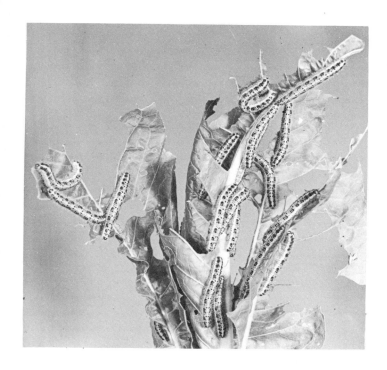

*The familiar
'cabbage' white caterpillars*

separated, a larva can detect other larvae by their smell and will follow trails of scent to locate colonies.

Within a few days of hatching the larvae will outgrow their first skin and make ready to shed it. They move an inch or so away from the feeding site and all sit together securely on their silk carpet. If examined closely at this time it will be noticed that the head appears to be falling off and the skin is shiny and stretched. Moulting is a critical period in the life of the caterpillar because not only is the old head capsule shed with the skin but so are the linings of the fore and hind guts. The old skin splits just behind the head and the larva pushes its way clear, drawing out its legs from the old skin as this shrivels back towards the rear end. The new skin is very soft and the larva must allow it to harden before it can move off to feed again. Moulting takes a few days to complete but the actual shedding of the skin is accomplished in ten minutes. Normally there are four moults during the larval life but there can be five under unusually low temperatures and only three if it is very hot. After the second moult the large white caterpillar assumes the black and yellow appearance by which it is most readily known. The conspicuous coloration is a warning to birds that the caterpillars are distasteful and this is reinforced by the unpleasant odour which they have. The caterpillars live in large colonies and expose themselves fearlessly on the surface of the leaves in marked contrast to the green well-camouflaged solitary-feeding caterpillars of the Small White which are readily eaten by birds.

*The parasitic wasp
'Apanteles glomoeratus' laying its eggs
in the caterpillars about to hatch*

Apanteles : the parasite

Caterpillar populations are kept in check by the action of predators, parasites and disease. The importance of these natural controlling factors should not be underestimated. From summer to summer the number of butterflies tends to remain steady, which can only mean that millions of surplus caterpillars are eliminated each year. Ground beetles, hover-fly larvae and spiders prey upon the larvae but they play a minor role in keeping down the numbers compared with that of the parasitic wasp *Apanteles*. This tiny insect lays its eggs under the skin of newly-hatched caterpillars and its larvae feed within the living caterpillar until they are ready to pupate. As many as 150 tiny parasites have been found in one caterpillar, but they feed on the fat storage tissues of their host, avoiding the vital tissues, so that the caterpillar itself continues to feed and grow. The growth rate of the parasite is synchronous with its hosts, and just as the caterpillar prepares to pupate, the parasitic larvae are also full grown. They find their way out by biting holes through its skin, and there alongside the dying host they spin a mass of yellow silk-covered cocoons. The female wasps locate host larvae by smell and have been known to find white butterfly caterpillars living on potted cabbages in a laboratory. *Apanteles* are themselves parasitised by an even smaller insect. Also they are easily killed by insecticides. But despite this they are possibly the most important factor in the natural control of large white butterfly numbers.

A possible means of control?

Insects are subject to many types of disease – from bacteria, fungi and viruses – and the large white butterfly has a virus disease which can kill them in their millions. The virus will pass through the egg to succeeding generations so that the disease can be spread over a wide area very quickly by a migrant species. The virus is

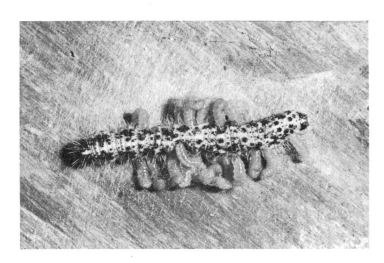

*'Apanteles' grubs emerging
from their still-living host*

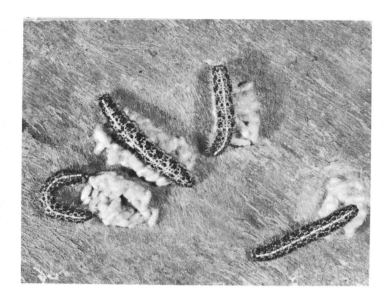

Silk cocoons spun by the wasp-grubs, inside which they will pupate

unlike those found in other animals in that it is able to withstand storage for long periods outside the insect tissues. It is specific to the caterpillars of the white butterflies, and could be as important in controlling this insect pest as myxomatosis was in rabbits. Since the appearance of the virus there have been no serious attacks of large white caterpillars; it is possible that the virus disease is the reason for this. It is true that there has also been an increase in the amount of insecticide used over the same period but it is certainly true that we are experiencing the longest-ever period without a white butterfly plague. In 1955 there were so many caterpillars in the Tamar Valley district that the railway lines were made slippery by the masses of crushed bodies!

Pupation

When the white butterfly caterpillar is fully grown it leaves the plant upon which it has been feeding and goes off in search of a suitable place on which to pupate. A caterpillar will travel some distance from the feeding area and will climb up a fence or building before preparing for the change into a chrysalis. The first action on finding a site is to spin a silk mat and a silk pad upon it as an anchorage for the chrysalis. Next, the caterpillar turns round and grasps the silk pad with its hind legs and proceeds to make a girdle by spinning silk from side to side over its back. The caterpillar rests for a day or two before shedding its skin for the last time and emerging as a firm inactive chrysalis. The colour of the chrysalis varies according to the background selected by the larva.

Chrysalids are very liable to be attacked by *Pteromalus*, a parasitic wasp. This tiny insect is unable to pierce the firm chrysalis

*Large white caterpillar
spinning girdle:
head away*

head towards

the silken girdle can clearly be seen

to lay its eggs inside, so it finds a larva which has spun the silken pad and girdle and sits alongside it until it changes into a chrysalis. When the chrysalis breaks out of the larval skin it is very soft and it only hardens after exposure to the air, so the little wasp climbs on to the newly turned pupa and inserts its eggs beneath the soft cuticle. The parasitic larvae feed upon the inside of the chrysalis, pupate and, at the time when the butterfly would have emerged, dozens of *Pteromalus* adults bite their way out of the chrysalis.

Birds eat chrysalids and blue tits will often be seen searching under fence rails and ledges during the winter. The extent of this predation may be judged by the number of butterflies found in sheds in the spring compared with those flying in the open. In Cornwall in the spring of 1948 following a white butterfly year there were very few butterflies to be seen on the wing but I found a closed shed with nearly a hundred butterflies trapped inside. Butterflies are not as successful in finding ways out as their caterpillars were in finding the way in.

The miracle of metamorphosis

The final transformation into the adult butterfly is fascinating and a continuing source of wonder to the observer. A few days before it is ready to emerge the miniature wings can be seen through the pupal case. The butterfly pushes forward in the chrysalis until it is burst open along the back just behind the head. By hunching the wings and struggling upwards, the plate covering the head, antennae and legs is pushed away and the butterfly can use its legs to draw itself clear of the chrysalis. The wings are only a fraction of their full size at this time and the butterfly expands them by pumping blood into the veins. The insect works frantically to achieve its perfect form, as the wings start to dry and harden as soon as they are exposed to the air. Within an hour the butterfly will be ready to fly and thus the life cycle of large white butterflies is completed.

In Britain there are normally two generations of large white butterflies each year, except in the north of Scotland where there is only one. In the very hot summers three broods have been known to occur. The principal factor determining the number of generations in a year is the length of the days when the young larvae are feeding. In the long summer days the caterpillars become pupae which emerge as butterflies within three weeks but the days are shorter when the next generation of caterpillars appears, and because of this the pupae which they form remain dormant and do not produce butterflies until the next year.

The Large White as a migrant

The large white butterfly is found throughout Europe, North Africa and Asia, in the north of India, and across to Japan. It is a famous migrant and countries at the north and south of its range

Chrysalis on fence post.
Note the area of the silken pad,
the girdle, and the
discarded caterpillar skin

are dependent upon these migrations to maintain the species there. Numbers of butterflies arrive in Britain every year from Europe and can be seen flying in across the sea on the south and east coast. Sometimes there are so many butterflies on the move that they look like a great cloud in the sky and the swarm will take hours to pass a stationary observer. In the last thirty-five years there have been six years when exceptional numbers have arrived and serious damage has been caused to cabbage crops. Observation of the flight of migrant butterflies has shown that the butterflies which arrive in Britain originate from northern Europe and move south-east into the Low Countries and across the North Sea. In France there is a continuing flight to the south-east but butterflies also move north and cross the English Channel to Britain. The most obvious migrations take place during the summer months but movement also takes place in the autumn and butterflies may be seen flying in the opposite direction. There is a southward migration through the Spanish Pyrenees in the autumn and in north India large white butterflies migrate up into the hills in the spring and down again in the autumn.

The next time a large white butterfly flutters into view, don't rush to the defence of your vegetable garden, but spare a thought for the marvel of its metamorphosis, the hazards which it has survived, or the distance it may have travelled to share the sunlight of the summer with us.

Known summer migration routes
of large whites across Europe

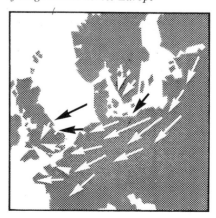

The Wandering Albatross *Lancelot Tickell*

To generations of seafarers the albatross has always been a long-awaited bird on voyages southwards towards the Cape and the Horn, as its appearance signals the end of calm tropical waters and the beginning of fresh breezes that eventually develop into the fierce westerly gales so characteristic of the great waters surrounding the Antarctic pack ice.

The southern hemisphere has the largest stretches of water in the world and seabirds are more numerous in the South Atlantic, Pacific and Indian oceans than anywhere else. From the deck of a ship the ocean often seems covered with birds as far as the eye can see, almost exclusively members of that great order of birds the Procellariiformes, which contains species adapted to all manner of marine conditions – the albatrosses, shearwaters, storm petrels and diving petrels. Of them all the wanderer *Diomedea exulans* (and its close cousin, the royal albatross *Diomedea epomophora*) are by far the largest, with a wingspan of ten to eleven feet.

It is not widely known that the ocean is a habitat which has been exploited by birds as thoroughly in their own fashion as by fish and other marine organisms. But although the true home of the albatrosses and other seabirds *is* the open ocean, no species has yet devised a way of reproducing at sea, and all must find some land upon which to nest and rear their young.

At sea in a strong wind the albatross is the lord of the elements, but the very shape which contributes so much to its mastery of flight in such conditions makes it ungainly and vulnerable on land. Consequently nests are found only on a handful of small islands scattered about the southern hemisphere. The most southerly island that they inhabit is South Georgia where the largest known breeding colony in the world is found.

In January 1775 when Captain James Cook first sighted South Georgia, believing it to be part of the great unknown southern continent *Terra Incognita Australis,* he came across a small island off the north-west tip of the mainland and called it 'Bird Isle on account of the large numbers that were upon it'. Over 180 years later when I landed in 1958 there were still large numbers, including four different kinds of albatross, and ideal conditions for studying them.

In midsummer (December) the lush grassy slopes of Bird Island are peppered with the gleaming white specks of wanderers.

'*At length did cross an albatross . . .*'

'*Pinking*' *an albatross on its*
nesting ground at South Georgia

A '*pinked*' *bird captured*
in winter quarters, New South Wales,
seven thousand miles
from its breeding area

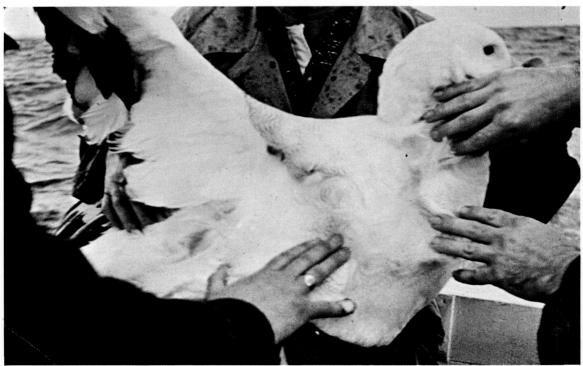

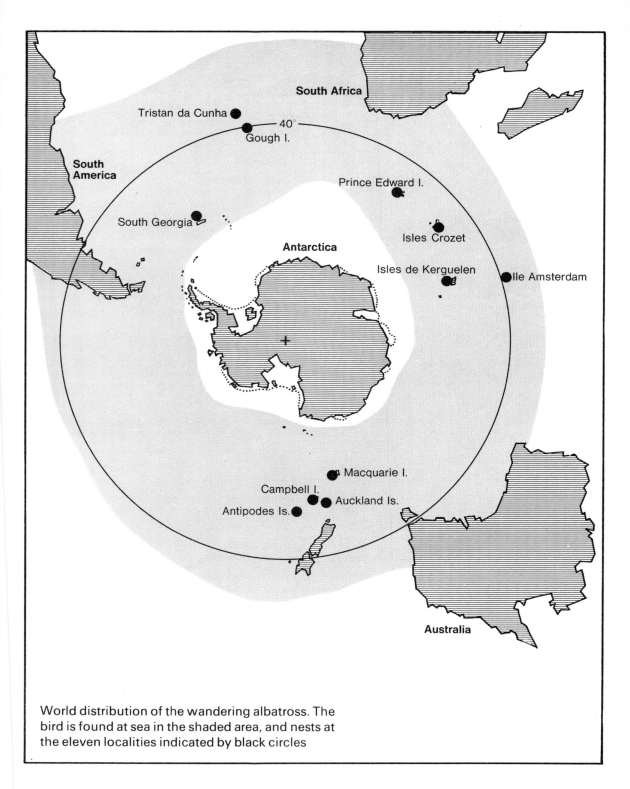

World distribution of the wandering albatross. The bird is found at sea in the shaded area, and nests at the eleven localities indicated by black circles

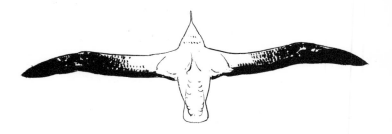

Designed for riding the westerlies,
a wanderer's wings
may carry it a million miles
in its half-century of living

Here and there the rough tussock grass gives way to flat meadows of moss and short Antarctic grass (called scientifically *Deschampsia antarctica*) just like scattered golf greens. In a very real sense these are albatross airfields and on days when the wind is slight the huge birds lumber around the perimeter to the downwind end before turning into wind for their run-off.

On the wing the bird is indeed impressive, but the too common description of the renowned bird tirelessly quartering the ocean upon unwavering wings is, like most superlatives, a little larger than life.

Flight and migration

The wanderer does flap its wings quite often, but that does not detract from the beauty of its movement. It is a soaring bird, but unlike the eagles and vultures which soar upon thermals, rising columns of warm air, the wanderer makes use of the fact that when wind blows over the sea, friction at the water causes air movement to be slower near the surface. If a wanderer dives from say fifty feet in calm air it increases speed. This speed is a form of energy that can be used to provide lift from the bottom of the dive just as a bicycle which freewheels down one side of a valley will climb part of the way up the other side. Like the bicycle, the albatross too would not return to the height it started from without propelling itself by flapping its wings. Calm days however are rare in the albatross latitudes and, when the bird dives downwind in a fresh breeze, not only does it build up greater speed, but when it turns into the wind and begins to rise it enters belts of faster-moving air, and therefore does not lose speed and can regain its original height without using its wings other than for adjusting balance. Following a ship a wanderer will make repeated dives to leeward, banking and returning to height abreast of the vessel or its wake.

In this way the wanderer travels thousands of miles each year throughout the southern oceans. During the last ten years, by marking albatrosses on the breeding grounds at South Georgia, we have been able to show that they are quite capable of circumnavigating the earth year after year, calling at distant feeding grounds on the opposite side of the globe from where they nest. Many of the birds ringed at Bird Island have been caught off the

New South Wales coast near Sydney, Australia, and then seen back home again at Bird Island. One notable bird ringed off New South Wales in August 1959 was found at Bird Island in February 1962 and then captured again in New South Wales in August 1962. We have no record of it in the summer of 1962–3, but it was back off Australia in July 1963 and had returned to South Georgia by the following summer, 1963–4.

Long before birds were ringed for scientific study seamen in the days of sail habitually caught albatrosses with baited hooks and released them with messages. On 30 December 1847 Captain Hiram Luther of the *Cachelot* shot an albatross in position latitude 43°S. longitude 79°W. Around its neck was the following message: 'Dec. 8th, 1847. Ship *Euphrates*, Edwards, 16 months out. 2300 barrels of oil, 150 of it sperm. I have not seen a whale for 4 months. Lat. 43°S. long. 148°40′W. Thick fog with rain.' In the twenty-two days between the time it was released from *Euphrates* and shot from *Cachelot* the bird had travelled 2,950 sea miles or 135 miles per day. This old record is still the best available evidence of the speed at which albatrosses travel.

The breeding cycle

Both the wandering and royal albatrosses take a year to complete a breeding cycle. The young albatross goes to sea for the first time exactly one year after it was laid as an egg and the parents who have been foraging at sea and bringing in food throughout the southern winter are in no condition to start nesting again straightaway, so they too leave the island just at the time when other adults are returning and laying.

The yearling wanderer is not white like its parents but black above with white face and underparts. The old seaman's name, gony, has long fallen out of use but it was one we found useful. As the young bird gets older the dark plumage gradually changes to white, but it may take twenty years for it to reach the final stage when all but the wingtips is white.

How an albatross flies.
In the diagram the arrows indicate
the direction of the wind.
The solid line is the course
of the bird marked on the
surface of the water, while
the dotted line indicates its
height above the sea

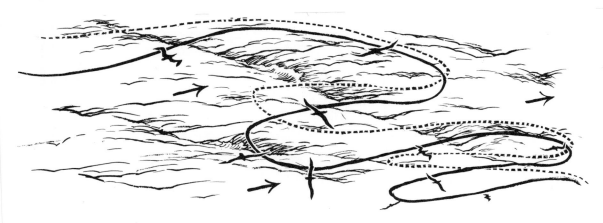

The young bird spends its early years at sea learning the marine environment and eventually returns about five years later to the island where it was reared. Although an experienced traveller at this age the five-year-old has had little social experience other than with its parents, and it spends another five summers visiting the island before finding a mate. At first it is very shy and just stands around occasionally making brief, wary attempts to approach another individual, but gradually it acquires confidence and associates with an apparently unattached bird. Over the years interest is narrowed down to one area and then one particular partner so that breeding is possible. These years could well be called 'dancing years', for the ecstatic ritual display of the wandering albatross has long been known as the albatross 'dance'. This behaviour consists of a series of territorial and appeasement signals, both visual and vocal, between a male and one or more females. When there are several females the male will set first to one then another. Any other male trying to attract one of the females will be vigorously driven off. The ritual reaches a crescendo when one or both partners stretch their wings outwards, and neck and head skywards, to the accompaniment of a series of loud, shrill screams, often ending in an aggressive attack. A rough interpretation of this would be that although the presence of the partner is desirable there is extreme anxiety about his or her close proximity. The establishment of the pair bond is accompanied by a reduction in the amount of this dramatic behaviour, until finally partners clearly recognise each other on sight and no longer have cause for anxiety. When together they spend a lot of time sitting quietly by each other, sometimes both simultaneously calling with a slow rhythmic *wa-wa-wa*, or preening each other's head and neck.

Mutual billing
by a pair of wandering albatrosses

Paradoxically the realities of breeding permit the partners to be together comparatively seldom, and then only for short periods. It seems that the function of the years of courtship is to create a permanent bond about which there is no uncertainty, allowing all energies to be devoted to the task of successfully rearing offspring.

Summer is well advanced by the time breeding birds appear on the island. Males come first and take up a nest position always within the same area. Occasionally it is upon the same site as a nest of a previous season, but it may be up to twenty-four yards away. About four or five weeks elapse between the arrival of the males and laying. During that period the male is at the nest three-quarters of the time, while the female appears for only an occasional day or so; for the rest of the time she is at sea feeding to produce the large egg, weighing about a pound. This arrangement is economical on the time and energy of both partners. The male selects the nest site, and his continued presence during the pre-egg period is not so much to defend the site – there is no shortage of sites on the wanderer breeding grounds – as to be available whenever the female appears. Copulation then occurs and the female learns where the nest is situated. The males are in full breeding condition when they arrive and in the absence of their own females have no hesitation in pursuing any passing female and forcibly copulating. Similarly a returning female walking to her nest and mate after landing may on the way be forced to submit to another male. The elaborate behaviour for intensifying the pair bond is evidently concerned more with later care of the young over the long fledgling period than with ensuring that copulation is exclusively between mated pairs.

Both parents contribute to the building of the nest, but the female alone is capable of building an adequate nest in a few hours before

Once the dancing has forged a pair-bond, the couple are faithful for the rest of their lives

Unlike almost every other known bird the female wanderer lays only every alternate year, not annually. From egg-laying to fledging is over twelve months

she lays; indeed a sure sign that an egg is about to be laid or has just been laid is a very dirty female vigorously tearing up turf and moss and placing it in a huge pile. Male and female share in rearing the offspring. The egg takes eleven weeks to hatch, and each parent sits alternately for periods that average anything from five to ten days, although the spells may be as short as one or as long as thirty-eight days. On average the male's shifts of incubation add up to slightly more than those of the female (forty-two days for males and thirty-eight for females). After hatching, the chick is still brooded by both parents for another four or five weeks, each partner spending about two and a half days at the nest at a time. At first the chick is fed a clear stomach oil, but within a few days it receives more substantial food and grows very rapidly. At hatching it weighs 300–400 grams, but within four or five weeks it has reached about six pounds and is left alone at the nest while both parents go off to sea to collect food.

When feeding chicks, parents generally forage within a range of about 200 miles of the nest. At South Georgia it was possible to determine this by colouring adults caught at the nest with a shocking-pink dye, and requesting ships in the south Atlantic to report positions of sightings. The wanderer is conspicuous enough at sea in its normal plumage, and colour makes it dramatically more so. Amusing reports reached us from the bridges of Royal Navy ships and whale-catchers which came across these psychedelic birds in mid-ocean!

The chick spends thirty-eight to forty-three weeks in the nest between hatching and departure, experiencing the full rigours of the sub-antarctic winter, from which it is protected by a thick layer of subcutaneous blubber and a dense coat of down. Throughout the winter both parents continue to visit their chick about once

Until the chick is a month old it is brooded by each parent in turn; shifts are of about three days

every three days, although often they are delayed, and a chick may have to wait up to three weeks between two feeds. Altogether, throughout the time the young bird is being fed the parents bring in a total of more than 130 lb. of food, mainly semi-digested fish and squid that is regurgitated by the adult and transferred to the guzzling youngster with surprising delicacy. By the time the coldest part of the winter approaches the chick has reached a peak weight of up to 33 lb., considerably more than that of the heaviest adults. This excess is lost during the final weeks in the nest. As summer displaces winter and the flight feathers of the young bird develop, it walks a lot in the vicinity of the nest to strengthen leg muscles, and exercises its wings frequently by jumping off the nest with wings extended.

Just at this time the coming season's breeding birds arrive and the year has gone full circle; one day when the wind is strong enough the young gony takes to the air and makes for the open sea. Once airborne there is no turning back. Parents too, freed from their feeding responsibilities, also depart.

A sub-adult wanderer

Breeding frequency

It is characteristic of the petrel family that only one egg is laid and if that is lost it is not replaced in the same season, i.e. the maximum reproductive potential is one offspring per year. The reproductive potential of the wanderer as we have seen is only half that, and furthermore breeding does not commence until the parents are almost ten years of age. From observations of individuals marked at Bird Island we know the rate at which albatrosses die from natural causes; it amounts to 4·3 per cent per year for both sexes, an extremely low death rate for a bird. Using this and other measurements of breeding success it is possible to construct a table of

The nibbling action of the chick stimulates the parent to regurgitate portion after portion of pre-digested sea-food

Netting a wanderer for ringing,
New South Wales

survival which tells us how long wanderers live, and the indication is that they are very long-lived. Sixteen per cent of eggs laid in any one year probably survive to ten years of age and 10 per cent to twenty years: theoretically there should also be 2·3 per cent still alive at fifty years. Obviously the principal reason that wandering albatrosses can afford such a low reproductive rate is that it has many years in which to raise young.

Biennial breeding poses another problem. Is it desirable, for instance, for there to be a balance between the proportion of the population nesting each year? We cannot answer this but there is a mechanism tending towards such a balance. At South Georgia more than half the breeding population nests each year, the over-lap being due to those pairs that lost eggs or early chicks in one season and were able to go to sea and get back in time for the following season. If all the eggs in an area were removed in one year then the whole breeding population would nest the following year and the numbers nesting annually thereafter would oscillate annually from year to year until equilibrium was reached after about ten years.

Man and albatross

In spite of the fact that few people have the opportunity to see an albatross, it is quite a well-known bird. A great many people who could not name a British seabird can say something about the albatross, for there is an old familiarity about the name evocative of stormy oceans and the misfortunes that can befall those who venture upon them; a tribute perhaps to the many schoolmasters who have laboured to pass on some of the magic of the *Rime of the Ancient Mariner* to bored classes. The poet, strangely enough, has had an even more profound influence upon man's attitude, for as the late Sir William Jameson has shown, the seaman's superstition that it is unlucky to kill an albatross originates directly from Samuel Taylor Coleridge's haunting verse. Before it became incorporated in the sailor's repertoire of superstitions, albatrosses were regularly killed by seamen for the welcome change they brought to a diet of 'salt junk' and 'hard tack'; moreover the birds were prized for their feet which were skinned to make fine tobacco pouches and for the long bones of the wings which made excellent pipestems. Modern ships travel too fast for albatrosses to be caught with the same ease as from slow sailing vessels and now that island-based sealing and whaling is rare, eggs are no longer taken in numbers from the breeding grounds. In a world where concern is felt for the future of so many less vulnerable species, it is pleasant to be able to report that the world population (20,000 breeding pairs) of the wandering albatross appears to be in a good state and anyone who undertakes a long sea voyage in the southern hemisphere is certain to see this magnificent bird.

*Doug Gibson
of the New South Wales
Albatross Study Group*

*Lance Tickell weighed each chick
in his study area daily.
He could tell whether
the young one had been fed
in the last twenty-four hours*

The Hedgehog *Patrick Morris*

In Britain the hedgehog (*Erinaceus europaeus*) or urchin is found almost everywhere, though it is scarce in mountainous regions, dense pinewoods and boggy areas. Unlike many other mammals, hedgehogs thrive in suburbia and indeed are often more numerous in gardens than in the open countryside. Why not? In towns there is plenty of shelter available, food is abundant in the form of scraps from bird-tables and dustbins, and of course many people treat their hedgehogs as free-ranging pets and put out food specially for them. The bustle of town life is no drawback and even in the central parts of London hedgehogs thrive, especially around parks and large unkempt gardens. A hedgehog once turned up in the middle of Chelsea, and another in the foreign mail section of the Admiralty in Whitehall!

The more normal haunts of hedgehogs are the edges of fields and woods, the patches of waste ground at the edge of towns, and of course the numerous hedgerows and bramble thickets in the countryside. It is here that we will pry into the private life of the hedgehog, beginning in late summer as it prepares for a most important annual event.

Hibernation

During the winter the hedgehog will be almost completely inactive, so all the food that it will need for the long months must be stored in its body in the form of fat. So in late summer and early autumn the hedgehog eats well and its weight goes up very rapidly. Soon it may tip the scales at nearly $2\frac{1}{2}$ lb., much of which consists of great wads of fat all around the body. (By the end of hibernation almost all the fat will have gone and the animal will have lost one-third of its weight – pretty drastic slimming!)

As the weather gets colder, the hedgehog becomes more and more predisposed to hibernate, and sometimes, if the weather is really bad, it may sleep for periods of several days. The hedgehog leaves its summer haunts and moves into winter quarters, often some distance away. Each animal constructs a winter nest for itself, usually sited underneath something which will provide support for the nest structure. Logs, bramble patches and garden sheds are favourite places. In the dead of night, with almost furtive secrecy, the hedgehog patiently shuffles about collecting dry leaves in its mouth. These are taken a few at a time and put into a pile at

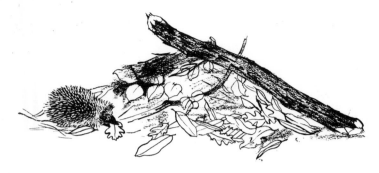

*Building a nest.
A pile of leaves collected under
a few strands of bramble and
twigs*

the chosen nest-site. More little bunches of leaves are added until quite a heap has been formed. The hedgehog then burrows into the heap and shuffles round and round inside until the leaves are packed tightly, lying flat against each other. The resulting winter nest is about eighteen inches in diameter and has a short entrance tunnel leading to the nest chamber. It is a carefully constructed affair and is remarkably effective in keeping out the wet and cold considering that it is only made of leaves. The thick, firmly packed walls of the nest remain waterproof for many weeks; they insulate the hibernating hedgehog from sub-zero temperatures and are surprisingly resistant to the normal processes that cause dead leaves to decay. A hedgehog's nest may thus remain in a serviceable condition for six months or more, but few are occupied for that long.

*The hedgehog burrows into the pile
and shuffles round inside*

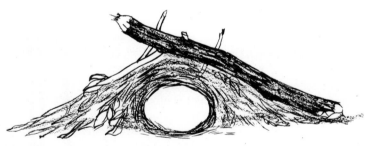

The typical completed nest

During winter the hedgehog remains snugly wrapped up in its nest, completely oblivious to all that goes on around it, for hibernation is not just a period of deep sleep, but involves the most fundamental changes in the hedgehog's physiology. The constituents of the blood change radically, the heart slows to one-twentieth of its normal rate, breathing may cease for several minutes at a time. Furthermore the hedgehog's whole body becomes stiff and cold and the structure of many of its internal organs is altered. These changes are so profound that the hedgehog is virtually switched off and cannot rouse quickly from hibernation; re-awakening may take an hour or more. But in this deeply torpid state the hedgehog is able to live without food or drink for several

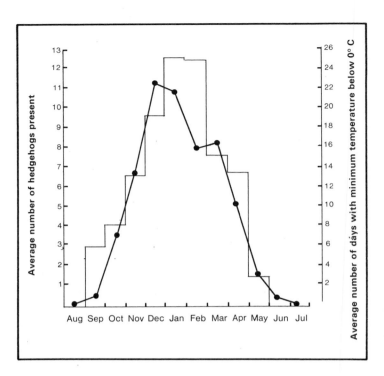

Diagram showing build-up of numbers of hedgehogs in winter quarters as weather gets colder in autumn, and reverse, as hedgehogs depart when weather gets warmer in the spring. The heavy line refers to the number of cold days, the light line to the number of hedgehogs

months. Tightly rolled up, it is protected from predators by its spines and from other hazards, like cold and melting snow, by its excess fat and the thick comforting walls of its nest.

The hedgehog just opts out of winter life and remains dormant in its hibernation nest for nearly five months, often longer in colder winters or more northerly latitudes. Contrary to general belief, the hedgehog does not just fall asleep about Guy Fawkes' Day and not wake up till Easter. The onset of hibernation is more the gradual result of increasing periods of inactivity as the weather gets colder, with the reverse taking place when the weather improves in spring. Again, contrary to popular belief, hedgehogs may awake several times during winter, perhaps to build a new nest or to feed; and hedgehogs are not infrequently seen even at Christmas-time. A hedgehog active in midwinter was once the subject of a court case!

With the coming of spring the hedgehog wakes up more frequently; by the end of April, when frosts are less frequent and there is no excuse for further inactivity, it moves out and takes up residence in its summer quarters, an area chosen for its food supply.

Breeding

During April and May the hedgehog is putting on weight very rapidly to compensate for the great loss of fatness over winter. Male hedgehogs get especially heavy at this time as parts of the reproductive system undergo enormous growth, sometimes half filling the abdomen, a state of flamboyant development unrivalled by any other mammal. The females also come into breeding condition at this time, and on warm evenings you may come across two hedgehogs 'courting'.

There is an old joke, 'how do hedgehogs mate, with all those spines?' The answer, 'rather carefully', is not far from the truth. Courtship manoeuvres are extremely protracted and often inconclusive. The male walks round and round the female, and she with dogged perversity shuffles round so as to remain facing him the whole time. Both keep up a continuous and very loud snorting noise that can be heard twenty or thirty yards away. This may go on for a very long time without consequence, and is most tedious to watch, but it must gain results sometimes, because by June many females are pregnant.

The young are born after a gestation period of a month or so and there are usually four or five babies in the litter. The newborn young are grotesque little things, all pink and grey with floppy ears. In a fortnight their eyes open, and a week later teeth begin to erupt. Each night the mother goes out in search of food and returns to suckle her babies in the family nest. If the nest is interfered with at this time the mother will often eat her young, but later on she is more likely to react by carrying them away one at a time, to a safer place. All the domestic chores are performed by the mother, the male hedgehog keeping well away from it all.

Three weeks after birth the young are quite lively and the

Baby hedgehogs remain with mother until they are about five weeks old and are led on foraging trips as a family group

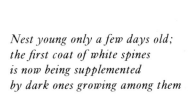

*Nest young only a few days old;
the first coat of white spines
is now being supplemented
by dark ones growing among them*

mother takes them out each night, in a shuffling family procession, to look for food, and then leads the babies back to the nest to sleep during the daytime. The most adventurous of the babies may begin to wander away from the family party, and at the age of about five or six weeks will finally cut the apron strings and go off to live its own solitary life. The other babies soon disperse too, perhaps driven away by the mother who can't be bothered to look after them any longer. Some babies seem to be reluctant to go it alone and there are stories told of 'lonely' hedgehogs adopting stiff scrubbing brushes as mother substitutes!

The spines

Having dealt briefly with the development of the young, it is worth making a digression to consider the hedgehog's most important and most obvious anatomical attribute – its spines.

Many books tell us that hedgehogs are 'born with soft white spines', but even a moment's thought makes this seem highly improbable. Regardless of what colour they are, or even whether they are hard or soft, the presence of any spines at all would be a distinct embarrassment to the mother during birth, especially if the baby was born back to front, as sometimes happens. In fact, when a hedgehog is born its spines are buried in the skin, but within a few hours the skin shrinks and the first set of soft spines (all white) appears. These are later augmented by further sets of spines (normal brown and white colours) which grow up among the preceding ones. By the time it leaves its mother's nest, a baby hedgehog is a real prickly piglet with nearly 3,000 spines on its back. This may increase slowly to about 6,000 or more in old hedgehogs. Spines are only modified hairs (a fact pointed out by Aristotle), and in most mammals the hair is moulted at least twice a year. Obviously the protective value of the spines would be much reduced if they were all suddenly moulted, so they simply lose the odd spine or two now and then. Replacement ones are growing all the time.

Each spine is about one inch long and full of air chambers to make it light but strong. One end is needle-sharp, but at the other end the spine forms a narrow 'neck' which is bent round and terminates in a large round knob. The thin, bent neck and rounded knob between them serve to prevent the spine being pushed back through the hedgehog's own skin. When it rolls up the hedgehog becomes a bristly, impregnable ball with its prickles pointing out in all directions. It rolls up so tightly that there is no opening and all parts of the body are protected; the spines are an unavoidable and painful deterrent to predators. So effective is this form of defence that the hedgehog probably has fewer natural predators than any other mammal of comparable size and habits. However, it is eaten by a range of animals including foxes, badgers and owls, but I suspect that these animals only take young hedgehogs that are not so adept at rolling up properly, or perhaps hedgehogs that have already died from other causes. It is a sad but true fact that nearly three-quarters of all hedgehogs born are killed by predators or succumb to the rigours of winter and never live to see their first birthday. It is often pointed out that the 'bristly ball' protection is highly effective against animal predators, but quite unsuited as a defence against motor-cars – hence the large numbers of squashed hedgehogs seen dead on roads. For millions of years, the hedgehog's skin was his castle, but not any more.

Home range and territory

To return to the hedgehog's activities in the summer months it is important to remember that, although it may indulge in the occasional daylight foray, sometimes even walking down streets among the shoppers, most of its private life is screened by darkness. Consequently we know little of the hedgehog's activities. For instance, to find out where it goes each night in its wanderings would entail following an inconspicuous animal in the dark, perhaps in thick vegetation, without disturbing it and without losing it – quite a task!

So, to try and find out a little about the hedgehog's summer activities, I used a technique developed in America – radio tracking. A hedgehog is fitted with a harness bearing a tiny radio transmitter (half the size of a matchbox) and this emits a continuous radio signal which can be detected using a suitable receiver. The radio-tagged hedgehog can thus be located at any time, and it can be followed about without being disturbed, even on the darkest night.

Already this technique has yielded some interesting results. The hedgehogs I studied moved from their winter-quarters to a different area to spend the summer. They appeared to have no rigidly

A baby hedgehog cannot roll up as tightly as an adult, and is thus more vulnerable to predators than in later life

Hedgehog carrying radio transmitter

defended territory; instead many animals tended to congregate in a particular area where food was abundant, and up to five could be found there at once. This was surprising in view of the hedgehog's pugnacious fighting behaviour, observed in captivity. When a fight does occur it is quite a comical affair, with two hedgehogs charging at each other, spines bristling, just like little clockwork toys scurrying about. After butting each other a few times, one hedgehog will give in and run away, leaving the other in peace.

Hedgehogs will eat almost anything edible found at ground level; they are particularly fond of worms

Lonely splendour: a nestling albatross in the sub-Antarctic winter

*A near-adult and a young wanderer
feeding on cuttlefish,
the principal natural food
in New South Wales*

The inquisitive hedgehog: notice its long nose, its small ears and eyes

Hedgehog removed from typical grass-and-leaves hibernating nest. The photographer was led to the nest by the snorting of its occupant

Since the radio-tagged hedgehogs could be located at any time, it was also possible to discover where the animals hid themselves during daylight hours. In fact they seemed to retire to the nearest patch of grass or other undergrowth, wrap themselves up and go to sleep. Few bothered to use elaborate nests of the type built during winter; by comparison, the summer nests were just temporary shelters where the hedgehog spent a day or two, but rarely any longer. On one occasion I was able to follow a mother hedgehog back to her nest where five young awaited her. How she managed to find the nest so quickly, over 300 yards away in thick vegetation, is a mystery. This study is only beginning and much more remains to be done. A major difficulty lies in the fact that hedgehogs are nocturnal and the investigator has to work all night as well as during the day. As a further drawback, I was twice interviewed by the police, regarding my suspicious behaviour, festooned with radio equipment patrolling the park at 2 a.m!

It is not really possible to say just how large a hedgehog's home range is. It must be greatly influenced by habitat; it is probably big where animals have to go a long way to find food. On the other hand, the hedgehog inhabiting a suburban garden could live under the potting shed and feed at the bird table or from a saucer at the back door and travel no more than fifty yards in a night.

Feeding

Animal books patiently list 'food of the hedgehog' but these accounts turn out to be no more than an inventory of the edible items found at ground level within the hedgehog's haunts. The hedgehog will in fact eat practically anything, and its teeth are well adapted to a mixed diet. Beetles are one of the main food items and the shiny fragments of these insects are not digested and remain clearly visible in hedgehog droppings. This is often a good way of telling whether nocturnal visitations to one's garden are being made by a cat or a hedgehog, when droppings are the only evidence. The hedgehog eats a lot of earthworms, presumably because these are easy to find, especially during damp summer evenings. The worms lie on the surface with part of their body still in their burrow. A quick grab by the hedgehog would simply snap the worm in two, but instead the hedgehog has a special worm-extracting manoeuvre. It holds the worm in its teeth and gently rocks backwards and forwards, easing the worm out of the soil until it has the whole thing.

No doubt the hedgehog will eat the eggs and young of ground-nesting birds, if it stumbles across them. Gamekeepers therefore regard them as a dire threat to their pheasants and partridges, and the shrivelled, prickly forms of many hedgehogs may be seen hanging on keeper's gibbets among the stoats and crows. People have pointed out that a pheasant's egg is too big for a hedgehog to tackle. Furthermore, if you give an unbroken egg to a hedgehog it does not know what to do with it. Against this, hedgehogs have actually been seen raiding nests (though the eggs may have been broken already). Anyway hedgehogs are traditionally regarded as vermin, and I know one estate where 20,000 have been killed in fifty years.

Closely connected with feeding are the old folk tales about the hedgehog carrying fruit impaled on its spines. This is a popular country story, even as far away as China. I have also seen a hedgehog carrying fruit depicted in a thirteenth-century manuscript, so the story is not new either. Another yarn is that the hedgehog will suckle milk from cows at night, a widespread story despite the fact that the hedgehog cannot open its mouth wide enough for the job. All I can say is that I have never seen either taking place, nor met anyone who has.

'Self-anointing' behaviour
is an energetic business.
The baby hedgehog produces frothy saliva
and throws it on to the spines
with its tongue

Hedgehogs often have hundreds of fleas burrowing among their spines; they are also carriers of ringworm and other diseases

Diseases and parasites

The personal hygiene of the hedgehog is perhaps one aspect of its private life we would do well not to investigate! The species has a well-deserved reputation for being flea-ridden; some individuals may carry several hundred of the parasites busily hurrying about among their host's spines. There are mites and ticks too, the latter sometimes fat and gorged with blood. The hedgehog never seems to care though; it makes little effort to clear itself of these dermal lodgers beyond scratching itself from time to time. To be fair, the most heavily infested individuals are often sickly and perhaps past caring anyway.

As for diseases, the hedgehog carries an alarming selection, including ringworm and foot-and-mouth. The former is transmissible to man, but is not very contagious. The latter is much more serious and its presence among wild hedgehogs could be an important factor during an epidemic on the farms.

Most of the hedgehog's diseases and parasites are not killers, nor is the species much troubled by predators as we have seen. Just what factors limit the population are not clear. Many hedgehogs die young, many more die in hibernation, as a result of accumulating too little fat to last through the whole winter. Vehicles also take their toll on the road. Hedgehogs seem particularly prone to falling into things too – fish-ponds and open manholes, for example, and I was once told of fifty-two hedgehogs that fell into a cattle grid!

Behaviour and senses

The hedgehog is famous for its extraordinary habit of 'self-anointing', a form of behaviour seemingly unique to the species. Stimulated by some special smell or taste, the animal will literally foam at the mouth, producing masses of frothy saliva which is thrown sideways and backwards by the head until it may look as though it is covered in soap-suds. The significance of this alarmingly energetic and somewhat messy performance is not clear.

*The 'defensive pose' in which
the hedgehog rolls up tightly,
tucking its head up against its tail
and hind limbs, so that the animal
is entirely wrapped up in its spiny skin*

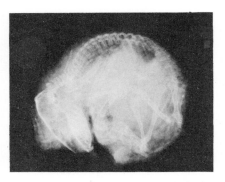

X-ray photograph of rolled-up hedgehog

Comparatively little is known about the behaviour of the hedgehog in its private life in the wild, and most behavioural studies have had to concentrate on captives. Hedgehogs will soon become tame and can even be trained to solve simple puzzles, explore mazes and so on. Observations and anatomical investigation show that the hedgehog places great reliance on its sense of smell. Hearing is quite good, but eyesight is poor. We may therefore imagine the hedgehog pottering about on warm summer nights, nose close to the ground to explore the olfactory kaleidoscope formed by the scent tracks of dozens of animals, big and small. Periodically the hedgehog may extract a worm or seize a beetle that did not run away fast enough, before continuing its meticulous search of the ground. Although not bothered by predators much, it is alert for the sight or sound of movement, and if startled will halt and hunch its body, bristling gently. If seriously threatened it will roll up tightly, and only relax when the coast is clear, ready to resume its night wanderings.

And so, come the autumn, with breeding finished, food getting scarce and nights getting cold, the hedgehog returns to its winter quarters. It may continue to forage on warm nights, but steadily becomes less active. Perhaps this winter, the physiological stress of hibernation may prove too much and kill it. Maybe, during its deep sleep, unable to react quickly and escape, it will be drowned in floods. Perhaps, too, it did not lay down enough fatty life insurance to tide it over the period of fasting and it will not have enough stored energy to last the long winter.

Hibernation is indeed a risky business. The lucky ones that survive will breed at about their first birthday and may reach a venerable seven years old, living much the same kind of life that hedgehogs have probably led since the miocene period, over ten million years ago.

The Starling   *Jeffery Boswall*

The starling *(Sturnus vulgaris)* is talkative, greedy, pushing, quarrelsome. He doesn't have to wait for opportunity to knock a second time, he's already there! The starling is probably the commonest and most successful wild bird in the world, and the secret of his success is opportunism. Some of the opportunities he takes don't exactly endear him to us but nevertheless his private life makes a fascinating story.

Our hero is not a large bird, about nine inches long. The starling's blackish plumage is shot with iridescent metallic colours, and in winter is also spangled with whitish flecks. In winter, too, the bill is horn-coloured, but for the breeding season it turns bright yellow, particularly in the male. Unlike many other birds about its own size which progress by hopping, the starling walks with quick, jerky steps, or it runs.

Thirty years ago James Fisher estimated that there were very approximately seven million nesting starlings (birds, not pairs) in England and Wales in early spring. Following a decrease in the early part of the last century, and extinction in many parts of the north and west of Britain, the starling then increased between about 1830 and 1880, recolonising many border areas and extending west into Cornwall and into western Wales. From then on the bird continued to increase and spread into the Scottish Highlands and Ireland and is still doing so. Even earlier, almost exactly two hundred years ago, Gilbert White, the gentle Hampshire curate, father-figure to British naturalists, wrote in his classic *Natural History of Selborne*, 'no number is known to breed in these parts.' Yet today scores of pairs must be nesting in Selborne each year.

Choosing a home

The commonest natural site chosen by the male starling in which to construct his nest is a crevice in a tree, or perhaps an old wood-pecker's hole. The species will also nidificate in the natural cracks of sea cliffs, or among rocks or heaps of stones. In Orkney and Shetland where there are virtually no trees I have found the birds occupying rabbit burrows on the ground. But today many sites, perhaps a majority, are man-made. There must be hundreds if not thousands of householders who complain of noisy starlings in their roofs. Yet there are also bird-lovers who put up nest-boxes to help starlings along!

Threat-song

Some starlings stay in pairs all the year round and keep in touch with their nest site, but this is not true of the majority. By late March an unattached cock starling will have made his final decision on a nest site for the year. Now he defends it with loud song and characteristic wing-waving postures. This double advertisement is usually enough. But should any contending cock starling prove really persistent in his take-over bid, he will be, to use the legal phrase, 'removed physically with as much force as may be necessary'. Unlike many other song-birds, the starling does *not* defend a large tract of land round the site; he dominates merely the nest-hole and one or two perches around. This difference probably relates to the fact that starlings sometimes breed in loose colonies, where stronger territoriality could hardly be exercised.

Early in April the still unpaired cock starts to collect material for the nest, and soon completes the main structure. It is usually rather an untidy affair with bits of straw poking out here and there, but doubtless it will function effectively: When the main shell is complete, it is ready to be offered to a potential mate in the vicinity. Likely females are lured into the general area of the site by a special *Kil-deeer* nest-advertisement call, and then chased or driven to the nest.

Pairing-up

Eventually one female accepts both nest and nest-builder, the birds become a pair and soon they'll mate for the first time. But before the initial sky-blue egg is laid, the hen must carefully line the nest with feathers and moss.

Five is the most usual clutch size. The eggs are laid daily and incubation starts with the arrival of the last one, so that they will all hatch together. At night it is always the female who covers the eggs; but by day the cock takes his turn enabling the female to feed, bathe, preen and so on. It will be almost a fortnight before the young break free of their shells.

One-man band

During his own off-duty periods the cock continues to sing. His extraordinarily varied and voluble song has been described by B. W. Tucker as 'a lively rambling medley of throaty warbling, chirruping, clicking and gurgling notes interspersed with musical whistles and pervaded by a peculiar creaky quality'. But more than all this, the starling is a mimic, an avian impressionist, taking off the songs of his bird neighbours. For a reason no scientist can confidently assert, the starling incorporates into his song the voices of other birds. In Wensleydale in Yorkshire, I have heard starlings mimicking the local moorland birds: lapwings, curlews and golden plover. And in Shetland they copy red-throated divers, fulmars and gulls. A Swiss bird-voice recordist was lucky enough to capture on tape a starling that wove into its song both the pure, high-pitched liquid notes of the golden oriole, and the harsh bass croakings of the common toad.

Farmstead starlings commonly copy the local hens, and I know of two cases where town birds faithfully reproduced the cries of distressed human babies. There is a reliable account in a scientific

One-man band:
the starling is a gifted mimic

journal of a starling that reproduced so effectively the ringing of a telephone bell that a lady gardener was lured into her house only to discover that she had been summoned by a starling perched on her chimney. I have been told that *after* the war in London some consternation was caused by birds mimicking doodle-bugs. An Irishman recounted to me a tale of how a football match outside Dublin had to be abandoned because there were two referees with whistles. One was running about the field in the usual way, the other was perched in a nearby tree. I cannot vouch for the veracity of either of these last stories, but would readily believe that they are true. An even more remarkable case concerns an Oxford starling that swayed and called like a bell it was imitating.

Vocal mimicry in birds is a mystery. Most other avian language can confidently be translated. Cock birds in normal song are saying 'This is my territory, others of my kind keep out!' Alarm calls are a mutual early-warning system when stoat or falcon threaten. Contact notes, used by night-flying flocks of migrants, are to keep the birds together. Chicks beg vocally for food, and nervous blackbirds at dusk have a rallying call as they gather to roost communally for the night. Mocking itself is such a well-established piece of bird behaviour that it too must surely have what biologists call 'survival value'. But no generally accepted explanation has been found. Some ornithologists believe that while the overall song style identifies the species, individual cocks are identifiable by the species they choose to mimic. My own belief is that we shall be driven to conclude that the birds enjoy playing with sounds, that they find it self-rewarding. There is mounting evidence that 'natural' song itself is not only functional but may also satisfy an aesthetic sense in the bird, evolutionarily anticipating man's own capacity for musical appreciation.

In addition to the purely voluntary copying that wild starlings do, captive birds will reproduce human speech rather after the manner of parrots, though less faithfully. In the BBC Sound Archive there is a recording of a caged starling saying 'Kiss me, cuddly, cuddly, cuddly, kiss me'!

New arrivals

May Day is as likely a day as any for the first clutch to hatch. Thus starts three busy weeks of food-finding for the parent starlings. But, busy though they'll be, their problems would have been worse at any other season because the whole breeding process is timed so that the young hatch when the maximum food is available. This is why starlings nest when they do. Just how they know when to start it is difficult to say, but increasing day-length is a factor.

The brood is visited anything up to 300 times a day with food. They grow quickly. A day-old starling will weigh $\frac{1}{4}$ ounce; two weeks later it will tip the ornithologist's portable scale at three ounces – twelve times as much. The sharing of the food operates by

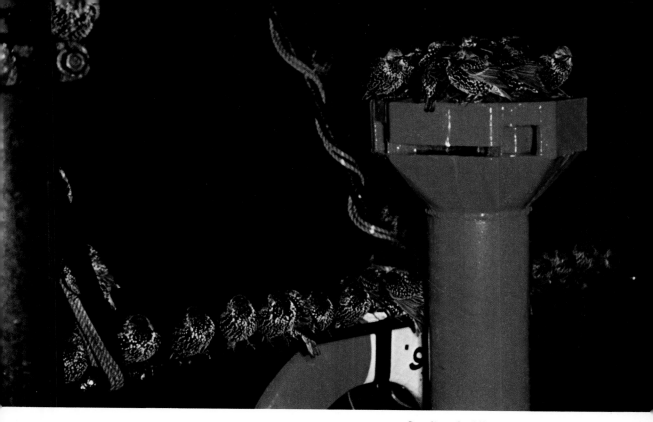

Starlings huddling together at night on the Smith's Knoll light vessel in the southern North Sea

A natural nest-site

Summer feeding

Winter feeding

a kind of internal audit. The hungriest chick fights hardest to get fed first, and always seems to succeed. But once fed it subsides and the next most hungry comes automatically to the head of the queue.

*Starlings in the roof
are a familiar problem*

Farmer's friend or foe?

The parents bring anything up to 1,200 sizeable insects or larvae a day to keep the brood going. Many of the creatures brought are of kinds known to be harmful to man's agricultural interests. Wireworms and leatherjackets, for example, both feed on the roots of cereal crops, so it is tempting to conclude that the starling must be a 'useful' bird. But is it? In one area of Scotland an ornithologist found that the local starlings fed their young almost entirely on leatherjackets. Each pair brought to its brood about 5,000 leatherjackets in three weeks. A great many leatherjackets, you would think. But what the scientist also found was that they were leaving behind, unmolested, between 92 and 95 per cent of all the local leatherjackets. So it looks as if, in this area at least, the activities of starlings have little effect on the total numbers of insect pests.

Empire-building

Had the early European settlers in foreign lands known that the starling was of little value as an agricultural ally, they would probably nevertheless still have taken starlings with them. The 'acclimatisation societies' of the day, as they were called, were motivated more by sentiment than practicality. Homesick emigrants introduced the starling to New Zealand in 1862 and the bird rapidly

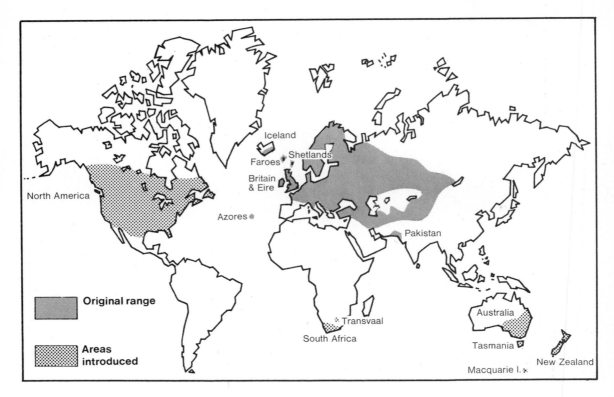

World distribution of the starling

colonised all the settled areas of both the north and south islands.
The early Australians followed suit the next year with thirty-six
birds; today the species covers not only half the island continent but
also Tasmania. The starling was introduced into South Africa in
1898, and once given a foothold by man, these hardy British
immigrants soon took most of the Cape Province by storm.

The most remarkable spread of all was in North America. An
eccentric who thought that all the birds mentioned by Shakespeare
should be allowed to live wild in the United States released eighty
birds in New York City's Central Park in 1890. Three-quarters of a
century later they have conquered a continent. Today, coast to
coast there must be something like 500 million starlings.

When populations build up to their natural ceiling on an island,
the surplus may attempt to spread overseas of their own accord.
Thus the New Zealand starlings have introduced themselves to
Campbell Island, 450 miles south of Dunedin, and even further, to
Macquarie Island, which may be regarded as a part of Antarctica!
Formerly a native only of Europe and a tiny part of Asia, the
starling's empire today extends to six of the seven continents.
Helped initially by man, this incredible creature must surely now
be one of the commonest and most successful wild birds in the
world. And in many of these colonial territories, as well as at home,
the numbers appear still to be increasing.

First flight

Once out of the nest, our family of five offspring will continue to be fed for a few days, but after that they will be on their own. They will join up in flocks with others of their own generation, while many adults embark on second families.

The wheezy cries of flocks of young starlings are typical of summer days in June. Mostly the birds forage on agricultural ground, often tailing along behind cattle and sheep that flush insect prey for them. Starlings will even perch on sheep's backs and relieve them of ticks, though this happens less nowadays when sheep are effectively 'dipped' against this particular infestation.

A favourite ploy in July is stealing fruit, cherries being perhaps the worst-hit fruit. The cherry orchards in Denmark of the Peter Heering company, makers of cherry brandy, manage to keep starlings off their cherries by broadcasting a recording of the injury call of a starling held in the hand. During eight seasons the method has proved 90 per cent effective. Previously, £1,000 worth of fruit was being stolen annually by *Sturnus vulgaris*.

Ant antics

In trying out different kinds of food, there comes a time when the young starling will meet ants for the first time. The young starling is still testing the edibility of various objects and one would suppose an ant might appear an attractive possibility. But the defence reaction of the ant is to squirt its own (formic) acid into the bird's face. Instead of retreating at once, the starling, by instinct, at once picks up the ant and, using it as a kind of living feather-spray, applies the acid to its feathers. The bird is literally

Starling 'anting'

anointing itself with an insecticide, the most likely purpose of 'anting' behaviour being to rid the plumage of feather-lice.

Toilet

Anting is only one aspect of feather care. Starlings also bathe, using distinctive movements. First, the front of the body is lowered into the water, the tail being held high, while the bird dips its head in and shakes its bill from side to side, all the while flicking its wings. Secondly, the bird lowers its tail end into the water and flicks its wings up and down, and then across its back. The aim is to wet the plumage evenly. But at the same time it must not become saturated, and this is avoided by constantly ruffling the feathers.

To help dry out, the bird shakes itself thoroughly. Next comes the oiling procedure. There is an oil gland above the base of the tail and, using its bill, the bird transfers the oil to most parts of the body. Some parts are more difficult than others though. Imagine trying to oil the top of your head with your bill! Having transferred the oil from preen-gland to bill, they then rub it off the bill with a foot and apply the foot to the top of the head!

No population problem

By the end of July second broods will be on the wing. By comparison with the April population, there will now be three or four times as many starlings in this country. Many young birds will already be dead because the immediate post-fledging time is a difficult period. By the following spring, many, many more birds are bound to die. We know this because the number of nesting pairs each spring is approximately the same from year to year. Thus, if in August there are two adults plus, say, two from the first

Starling bathing

brood and three from the second, that will be a total of seven birds. By the following April five out of these seven *must* die. British-bred starlings do not migrate. How most of them die is not known, but it is clear that in midwinter there is a pinch-period when temperatures are lowest, food scarcest, and daylight hours in which to forage are also at a minimum.

Most animals produce a surplus when they breed and all populations are naturally regulated and avoid over-population. All, that is, except one. The naked ape himself is the one species that has lost the ability to keep its numbers within reasonable control.

Immigrant problem

To return to our over-wintering starlings, their problem can hardly be eased by the arrival from the continent each autumn of hordes of immigrant starlings that pour in across the North Sea.

Starling 'sunning'

In 1953 I organised a special piece of research to study these overseas migrants. Bird migration had attracted many followers, both amateur and professional, in post-war Europe. Much was being learnt of the inland and coastal paths followed by birds on their annual journeys. But comparatively little was known of their behaviour when flying over featureless, inhospitable areas such as the North Sea. The Smith's Knoll light-vessel, twenty-five miles off the coast of Norfolk, was manned by us from mid-September to mid-November.

Easily the commonest diurnal migrant was the starling, a bird known for some reason to the lightmen as the 'Jacob'. Tight black battalions trooped past with uncanny steadiness of course on a south-westerly bearing. Two birds caught on board bore rings on their legs. One had been marked as a nestling in Sweden the previous June, the other, also as a young one, in the Soviet Union. These 'recoveries' of ringed starlings, along with many others over the years, show that the areas of origin of winter visitors to Britain are mainly Russia, Finland, the Baltic States and Germany. There the winters are much more severe and the birds have to move out westwards to the more maritime climate of the Atlantic seaboard.

The starling migrates by night as well as by day. And this fact gave us the opportunity to catch and ring 700 birds ourselves while on board the Smith's Knoll lightship. When moving in darkness they navigate by the stars. But if the heavens are blotted out by overcast cloud or by fog, then they are attracted by the powerful beams of the lightship lantern.

I shall never forget the night of 17–18 October 1953. There was a low cloud base and light rain. Thousands of birds descended on the ship, seeking resting places, and thousands more circled round and round the lantern, flying in the beams of the light. Chaffinches and skylarks were roosting on the deck machinery and ship's rail, heads tucked into scapulars. Many were so tired that it was possible

Starlings roosting on Admiralty Arch, central London

to pick one up, put a ring on its leg and replace it in the same position. Starlings were more restless and tended to perch in the rigging. Some of them could be caught as they fluttered down after hitting the lantern glass. But the best method was to go up on to the lantern gallery itself, a hundred feet above the sea. There, using a long-handled net, one could lean out into the night and hook starlings from the sky. It was a tremendously exciting experience. The crew and I were up all night. We caught and ringed a total of 354 birds, most of them starlings. One subsequently turned up in Norfolk, one in Kent and two in Wales.

The mortality that results from a night visitation is terrific. Bucketfuls of birds are picked up in the morning and thrown overboard to the waiting gulls. The ship also looks as if it has had a coat of whitewash. 'Them bloody Jacobs,' the lightmen would say; and, turning to me: 'You're a bird-watcher, it must be *your* fault. The Jacobs only came to see you!'

Town dormitories

In winter both resident and immigrant starlings are dispersed across the British countryside in flocks. Each flock is perhaps a few hundred birds strong. By night the flocks assemble by the hundred thousand.

The best-known roosts of starlings are those in towns. Fifteen British cities are used as dormitories by large numbers of starlings. The biggest assemblage by far is Glasgow where there are at least a quarter of a million birds. They collect on old buildings in the centre of the city, which have earned the title 'whited sepulchres'.

In London 100,000 commuting starlings change places each morning and evening with the human commuters. The well-known London Transport tube map has been matched by a comparable piece of cartography to show the routes taken by starlings. It's the work of the ornithological section of the London Natural History Society and it shows fly-lines, some of which have been in use for thirty years. Others, like the Victoria Line, are newer. The most distant feeding grounds are fourteen miles from the West End, but the majority of birds feed in the more immediate suburban gardens, breaking up into small flocks for the day.

The black blizzards that come sweeping in to the city ledges have caused considerable public concern. Buildings are fouled, and special bus shelters have had to be built. There has been constant agitation from property owners, complaints from the public – even questions in the House of Commons. On one classic occasion so many starlings perched on the minute hand of Big Ben that they prevented nine o'clock from being struck.

The Ministry of Works and various local authorities have fought a thirty-years' war against the starling. They are still campaigning! Birmingham City Council has tried as hard as any to shift the birds. A stuffed owl on masonry on a civic building only served as a comfortable perch. Rubber snakes, said to have been effective in the United States, were treated with similar disdain. A supersonic siren proved reasonably effective but was even more distressing to humans than were the birds. Fireworks are also more of a nuisance than the birds themselves. A double electric wire can be effective but is expensive to install and demands maintenance. A

Hurrying in to the roost site

broadcast recording of a starling's distress cry worked initially, but the effect soon wore off. Another method is to apply to ledges a strip of plastic gel known as 'scarecrow strip' which is laid as a continuous ribbon. This was apparently done with some success at the National Gallery. The makers claim that alighting birds feel a sense of insecurity and fly away. The preparation is said to last at least twelve months. Some, who agree it works, describe it as a very successful method of shifting birds on to the buildings opposite!

Country residences

Another rearguard action in the aerial war against the starling is being fought in the country. Roosts may house a million birds or more and droppings can quickly defoliate and even on occasion kill trees. Unlike in the town, in the *country* the broadcasting of distress calls can in certain cases – but not all – shift a roost. In cases where a real threat to valuable timber can be demonstrated, and where success is considered likely, the Ministry of Agriculture will send a Regional Pest Officer along to clear a roost. Based on original research in France and America, this acoustic scaring method is probably more advanced here than anywhere else in the world. A recording of a starling yelling blue murder is played at just the right moments. Often a wood can be cleared in two evenings but it is as well to be about for the next two or three nights in order to provide an added deterrent. It must be emphasised that only roosts in certain kinds of situation and of a certain size can be cleared in this way. But of those attempted the Ministry have cleared more than 90 per cent.

The foal is only twenty minutes old and yet able to stand

New Forest ponies eat almost anything

Mare and her yearling at the
Beaulieu Road Sales

Some country roost sites are known to have been occupied for more than 250 years. Starlings are known to have been coming to the reed-bed at Slapton in Devon since 1797. The biggest roost estimated in Britain is of three million birds in Norfolk. To witness the assemblage of these birds is the most impressive sight the British bird-watcher could offer to anybody. It is a 'sunset spectacular'. A large roost will have a catchment area of up to thirty miles in diameter; as the sun sets the birds come hurrying in, flying at perhaps 40 miles per hour. The roosting procedure is accompanied by excited community-singing, alternating with bickering and rivalry over perching places. Then suddenly the whole company rises with a great roar of wings to engage in the most impressive aerial manoeuvres. The multitude changes shape and direction like a huge writhing animal silhouetted against the sky. On the grand scale, these aerial evolutions are one of the great marvels of animal adaptation, so perfect is the birds' co-ordination.

Why exactly the birds travel such distances – even in midwinter when energy is short – to assemble, isn't really understood by scientists. Could it be safety? A recent suggestion is that the birds, in effect, hold a nightly 'conference' about their own numbers in relation to the local food supply and that, if food is running out, a percentage of birds has to move on. An alternative and perhaps more viable theory is that the roost acts as an information centre

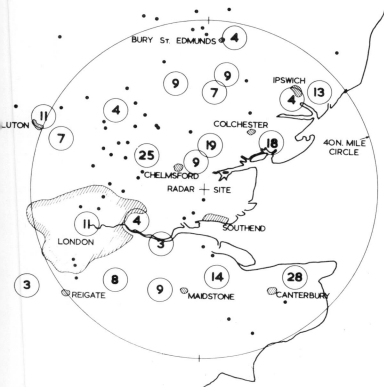

Geographical distribution of ring-angel centres, 1959, i.e. of starling roosts. Some of the ring-angels derived from sources proved to be active on several occasions during the year, and these are plotted as large open circles. (The number within the circle corresponds to the number of observed starling dispersals.) A few ring-angels were observed on one occasion only and the small solid circles show the location of these sources

145

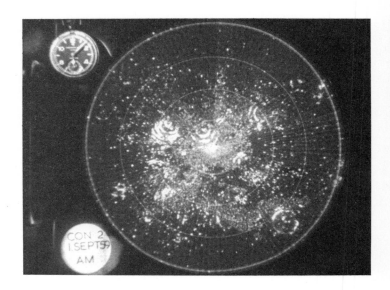

*Radar ring-angels
observed on 1 September 1959,
produced by the dispersal of starlings
from their roost at sunrise*

telling birds where food is available. The idea is that the birds that have fed well the previous day may leave the roost more purposefully in the morning to return to the favourable locality. Those that have fed less well would join those groups whose behaviour indicates that they are heading for an area where food is to be had.

The evening activities last perhaps thirty minutes or more, depending on the season, before the last bird drops to its perch. In midwinter this is usually a little before sunset. In midwinter starlings rise early. They are not easy to see, but, surprisingly enough, a particularly revealing picture can be got by looking at a radar screen. At the Marconi radar station on the top of Bushy Hill in Essex, the morning departures can clearly be seen as radiating ripples of dots. All unidentified dots were originally dubbed 'angels' by the radar men. The angels were subsequently discovered to represent birds – another kind of winged biped! Dots in circles that move outward like ripples on a pond are known as 'ring-angels'. A radar view of the whole of south-east England early in the morning shows starlings dispersing simultaneously from many roosts.

Starlings go home!

At dawn on 1 March one year we suddenly find that the ripples don't appear any more. Instead of fanning out radially, the birds are surging eastward. The continental cousins are going home to nest. Back home our own birds take up their own song-posts, several million cock starlings starting the cycle over again.

The New Forest Pony *Stephanie Tyler*

The New Forest Ponies (*Equus caballus*) are one of nine breeds of semi-wild ponies that are to be found in the British Isles. They have been recorded in the New Forest since early Norman times but their numbers were small until the mid-nineteenth century. Until then grazing areas available for ponies and cattle were restricted because of the overriding importance of maintaining large deer herds for royal hunts. After the Deer Removal Act of 1851 most of the deer were killed and the number of ponies was then able to increase; there are now over two and a half thousand ponies in the forest.

The ponies are all owned and controlled by the holders of common rights in the New Forest and each must be branded with its owner's mark. Most of the adult ponies are mares because the number of stallions over two years of age is kept at about 120 and these selected stallions must be passed each year as fit to run on the forest. Their number is further reduced in the winter when many are taken on to the farms and smallholdings. Each autumn there are round-ups to catch the foals born in the previous spring and summer. Most of the colts are then taken from their mothers and sold at the annual Beaulieu Road Sales. Some filly foals and older animals may also be removed and sold, but the remaining foals are branded and released.

Despite the great control exerted by man, the ponies do lead an almost wild existence. They have to find their own food, except in hard winters when hay may be provided, and they have few restrictions on their movements. Fences have been erected along two main roads running through the forest in an attempt to reduce the numbers of ponies and cattle killed by motor vehicles, and though these fences may seem to restrict the ponies' movements, they can cross from one side of a fenced road to the other by underpasses.

Composition of the pony groups

To the average visitor in the New Forest these ponies may seem to lead an aimless existence but they are in fact divided into highly organised units with fixed ranges and habits and lead complex social lives. Ponies do not wander on their own or at random over the whole forest but instead are associated into small

It is necessary to give the ponies hay during prolonged snow-fall

groups. These groups, if left undisturbed by man, are generally very stable from year to year and each remains in a small area of up to four square miles. Many of the groups are basically family units consisting of one adult mare and one or more of her own young offspring; others consist of two adult mares with some of their offspring, and, more rarely, of up to eight mares. A very few mares appear to be solitary but this is usually because their foals or yearlings have been taken from them.

Most of the few stallions allowed on the forest throughout the year become attached to particular mare groups. This arrangement closely parallels the way in which another member of the horse family, the steppe zebra, makes up its groups. These zebras also go about in small parties of one adult stallion, two to six mares and their immature offspring. The scarcity of stallions in the New Forest, however, results in most pony groups being unaccompanied by males, and bachelor groups of surplus young stallions which are commonly seen in zebra herds do not occur here at all.

Adult mares in a group usually stay together for many months, while immature and young ponies do change groups. Young fillies generally leave their mother's group when two, three or four years old, by which time they are sexually mature, and they eventually join up with another group or with another single mare, or remain on their own to form the basis of a new family group. Few colts are left in the forest after their second autumn but it seems that of those allowed to remain most voluntarily leave their mothers at about the age of three.

Mutual grooming

Mutual grooming, where two ponies face each other and then nibble each other along the neck and withers, is a common form of social contact between group companions but, except between immature ponies, it only rarely occurs between ponies from different groups. When it does it is often an indication that the animals involved are related or that they once belonged to the same group. Even within a large group, each mare usually has a preferred grooming partner and will only infrequently groom with other ponies.

Hierarchies

A rigid hierarchy exists between members of any group and between ponies from different groups that regularly come into contact. A dominant mare will lay back her ears and threaten to bite or kick a more subordinate mare in her group that approaches too closely. The subordinate animal will then quickly move away without returning the threat. Few fights therefore occur in the competition for food, water or space, except when two mares from strange groups meet or when one mare is trying to change her order of rank and gain 'promotion'.

Age is very important in determining a mare's rank: young animals are usually at the bottom of the hierarchies and older animals at the top. However, amongst old mares sheer body size is more important than actual age, and so large mares tend to be dominant over smaller mares of similar age. Sometimes temperament may also be of great importance as a few small, young but very aggressive mares may on occasion dominate much larger and older ones.

Mutual grooming between a mare and her three-month-old foal

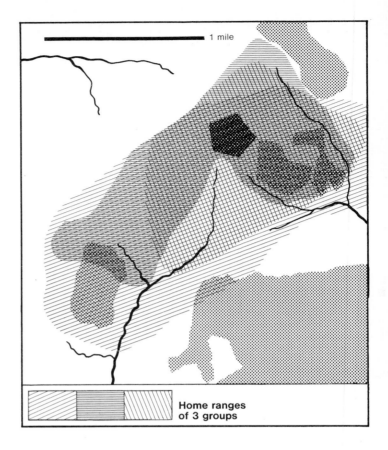

1 mile

Home ranges
of 3 groups

*Home ranges of three groups
showing the size
and the great degree
of overlap of the ranges.
The stippled areas represent
woodland and the dark
patch is a reseeded area*

Stallions are usually dominant over all mares in competition for food but in some other situations, such as when a mare has a very young foal, mares may even bite or kick stallions. Hierarchies also exist between the stallions themselves and, as with mares, old, large animals are dominant over younger, smaller males. The age and strength of a stallion also determine the number of mares that he can keep together during the breeding season.

Although any member of a group may move off first, the dominant mare of that group soon takes over the lead when the group is travelling purposefully. The rest of the adult members of the group follow in single file according to their order of rank, but immature ponies follow their mothers in their ascending order of age. So in a group consisting of two adult mares each with a foal and yearling, you would expect to see the dominant of the two mares leading with her foal following closely behind her or at her side. Her yearling follows the foal; after the yearling walks the second mare followed by her foal and then by her yearling who brings up the rear. In groups to which stallions are attached the stallion very rarely leads but usually walks behind his group as do zebra stallions. When ponies are alarmed, the single-file movement breaks down and group companions quickly bunch together and gallop alongside one another.

The home ranges

Any one group remains within an area of some one to four square miles. This area, which is remarkably stable from year to year, is not defended against other groups and so constitutes a home range rather than a territory. The home ranges of different groups overlap considerably; they may even be almost identical but in such cases the groups involved have their own preferred parts of the grazing areas within their ranges and so are still to some extent segregated, particularly in the winter.

Contrary to what one might expect, larger groups do not have larger ranges. The nature of the habitat is more important than its actual area. Four main requirements must be found: sufficient food, water, shelter and a 'shade' for the summer months. Where these four requirements are met with in a small area, the home ranges of groups in the area are small; but where large tracts of unproductive heathland separate a good grazing area from the shelter of valleys or woods or from water, the home ranges are correspondingly large.

Patterns of movement in the home ranges

The way the animals move about is influenced by the season and by the time of day. Within home ranges it is often possible to predict where a particular group may be found at any time of the day or year. Certain parts may be used in only one season or even one month of the year. The majority of pony groups in the forest spend the day on open grazing areas such as woodland clearings,

Up to a hundred ponies made up of several groups may be seen using the same 'shade' at one time

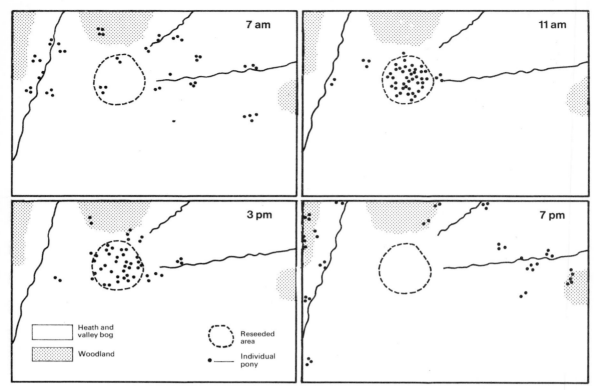

7 am

11 am

3 pm

7 pm

Heath and valley bog

Woodland

Reseeded area

Individual pony

The diurnal pattern movement of ponies as typified by one day in December. Each dot represents the position of an individual pony

streamside lawns or reseeded areas. The presence of a restricted number of such large favoured grazing areas results in recognisable 'groups of groups', with each super-group centred on one of the grazing areas.

The daily patterns of movement shown by groups belonging to any of these super-groups are very similar. Soon after dawn most groups move on to their grazing area and usually remain there until the evening when they return to the more sheltered woods and valley bogs. Strong winds or rain may cause the ponies to remain in the shelter of the woods and valleys throughout the day or at least affect the amount of time that they remain out on the grazing areas. Hot, calm weather in the summer also affects the pattern of movement by causing the ponies to move quickly to 'shades', where they remain during the hottest part of the day to avoid the irritation from numerous species of flies. Some 'shades' are in true shade such as under trees or in railway tunnels but others are in the open on crests of hills or on patches of concrete where air currents probably reduce the number of flies. All the groups of a super-group generally use the same 'shade', so that up to a hundred ponies may sometimes be seen standing closely together under a group of trees. Because of the communal 'shades' the home ranges of different groups in a population show more overlap in summer than in winter.

During the winter ponies graze, or browse gorse and holly, for much of the day. Sometimes they graze almost continuously from dawn to dusk but usually they take one (or more rarely two) rest periods. For adult ponies this is usually taken late in the morning and lasts on average for just over half an hour. The ponies also feed almost continuously throughout the night in both winter and summer, although in summer, when food is more plentiful, the ponies can spend longer periods resting during the day; between June and September they may even rest for five or six hours at a time in the 'shades'.

The foaling season

The foaling season usually begins in late March and finishes by September with the majority of births in May. Very occasionally a mare may foal when only two years old but most do not have their first foals until they are three or four. As the gestation length for

Variations in time of resting, dependent on weather conditions and the season.
Feb. 2nd Sun broke through the clouds at 10 a.m. and this resulted in a resting peak at 12 noon
Feb. 8th Overcast throughout the day
March 29th Sky clear from dawn
July 2nd Hot, calm and sunny. Ponies rested in a 'shade'
July 18th Dull, cool day
Sept. 27th Sun broke through clouds at 7.30 a.m.
Nov. 7th Overcast throughout the day
Nov. 9th Sky clear from dawn

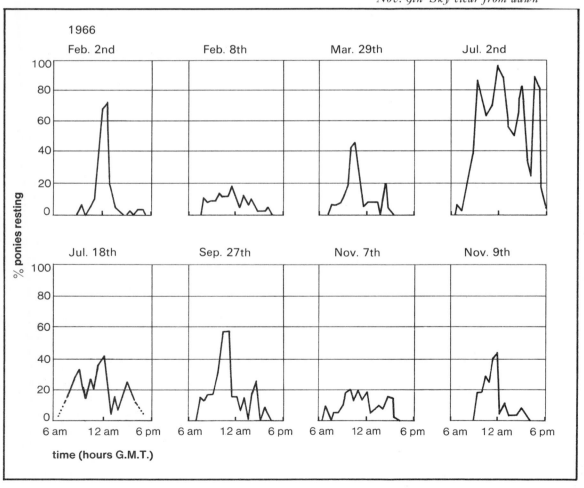

*Immediately after the birth
of her foal the mare starts licking
it, which helps to establish
the mother-baby bond*

ponies is about eleven and a half months, and as mares usually mate within about nine days of foaling, they may in theory foal every year until their death – usually before the age of twenty. In practice, however, very few mares do foal each year; most produce one only every two to three years.

Immediately before parturition, mares leave their group companions and any offspring that they may already have, and seek a quiet sheltered spot. There are exceptions: a few mares foal out in the open surrounded by other ponies, or even at the side of a busy road surrounded by human spectators.

The birth is short – it is usually completed in thirty minutes – and within an hour a normal foal can stand and suck. The mare licks her new foal intensively during its first hour; this licking seems very important in enabling her to learn to recognise its smell.

Soon after a mare has suckled her new foal she takes it back to her group. However, she keeps very close to it during the rest of its first day and shelters it from all other ponies, manoeuvring herself between the foal and any other pony and then leading the foal away. She also threatens any subordinate pony that approaches her new foal and will even threaten her own yearling. These efforts are essential for the normal establishment of the mother-foal bond, because newborn foals will tend to follow any large moving object, even a car driven slowly past them. Sometimes a young foal may even become attached to a stationary object such as a tree and refuse to follow or suck from its real mother. For these reasons the real mother must ensure that her new foal stays close to her until it is able to recognise her. After this critical period during a foal's first day, the mare will then allow her yearling to rejoin her and will henceforward spend much less time protecting her foal from other ponies.

Mares are very aggressive to foals other than their own; they will even bite or kick strange day-old foals, but young foals soon learn to avoid them. Although no mare will normally suckle a strange foal this can sometimes be brought about artificially by draping the skin of a mare's dead foal over a strange one. This practice, commonly adopted by shepherds, depends on a mother's ability to recognise the smell of her own young. A long period of enforced contact during which a mare is prevented from kicking a strange foal may also eventually lead to her accepting it as her own. However, both these methods are more effective if the mare has only recently foaled.

Young foals spend much time resting, roughly half the day until their fourth month, but even on their first day they may be seen nibbling or chewing grass and twigs. The time spent grazing increases gradually up to their fourth month and more rapidly thereafter. Foals continue to be suckled for about a year, to within a few days or weeks of their mothers foaling again. If a mare does not foal the following year, she may continue to suckle her yearling and occasionally two- or three-year-old ponies may still be seen sucking from their mothers.

Play

The play of very young foals is centred around their mothers; they gallop to and from them or in circles around them and rear

Mare suckling her week-old foal

up at them, or chew and pull their manes, legs and tails. When three to four weeks old, they become more independent, and move further from their mothers, showing an increasing interest in other young foals with whom they then spend long periods playing throughout the summer. Differences between the play of colts and fillies soon become evident. Play between colts is rough and takes the form of fights whereas fillies merely groom together or occasionally chase one another. When a colt grooms a filly he quickly becomes too rough and bites at her neck and legs, frightening her off. Colt foals will play-fight with colt yearlings or even with adult stallions, who are much more tolerant of foals than are mares. All forms of play are rare in the winter when food is scarce, and energy presumably needs to be conserved.

Fights between stallions and formation of 'harems'

In the spring stallions fight amongst themselves to establish ownership of the groups. When two stallions of similar strength are present on the same area, they usually share out the groups between them and may each own up to about fifty mares. Fights then occur only when a mare belonging to one of the stallions moves towards the other stallion. The first gallops after her; he has a brief ritualised fight with the second stallion and then with

Stallions fighting

his head lowered drives the mare back to join the rest of his 'harem'. After such a fight each stallion generally rounds up all his mares into a tight bunch. Otherwise they are spread out over the grazing area, with each stallion grazing close to his one favoured group unless a mare from another of his groups is in oestrus.

Stallions have no geographically defined territories and they will even stand peaceably, a few yards apart in the 'shades'. Their 'harems' of mare groups do to some extent constitute moving territories but these 'harems' are not constant. In the evenings the different mare-groups making up a 'harem' usually leave the grazing areas separately for the valleys or woods and so each spends the night with only one or two groups. Moreover, if one stallion is late in returning to the grazing area in the morning, the second stallion may copulate with a mare belonging to the first stallion. This is in contrast to zebras where each stallion copulates exclusively with the few mares in his own group.

By September the foaling season is over, and most mares have been served by the stallions, who then cease to defend their 'harems' from rivals. 'Shading' also ceases and individual mare-groups come less into contact. All the ponies left out on the forest must devote their time to grazing and browsing if they are to survive until the following spring.

Biographical Notes

Jeffery Boswall was formerly on the staff of the Royal Society for the Protection of Birds, and was the first new producer to join the BBC Natural History Unit after its formation in 1957. He was the producer and writer of *The Private Life of the Kingfisher*. Happiest as a director-cameraman with his eye to the viewfinder, he was recently made an Associate of the Royal Photographic Society with his films *Bleeding Hearts and Bone-Breakers* and *Everyman's Antarctica*.

John Morton Boyd was educated at Kilmarnock Academy and read zoology at Glasgow. A thesis on the ecology of earthworms gained him a Ph.D. In 1957 he became the Nature Conservancy's Regional Officer for West Scotland, an area that holds more grey seals than any other in the world. He is now Conservation Officer, Scotland, but is still able to take time off from high-level policy-making to indulge his passion for island-going. He is probably the only man alive to have landed on all the major islands and sea-stacks of the St Kilda archipelago.

Roger Burrows read biology and geology at the University of Keele. He taught biology to school-children, and extra-murally to adults. He is currently warden of his own Breanoc Field Centre at St Agnes on the Cornwall coast. His particular interests are sea-shore life and mammals. His book, *Wild Fox*, was published in 1968.

John H. D. Hooper has a degree in chemistry, is a Fellow of the Institute of Petroleum, and works, near his home in Staines, in the Research and Technical Development Department of a major oil company. He is married with one daughter. He and his wife, Winifred, have long been interested in spelaeology and have done much exploration and survey of caves in Devon. In 1948, with other members of the Devon Spelaeological Society, which they helped to found in 1947, they began a study of cave-dwelling bats in Devon, and undertook the first large-scale bat-banding experiment in Britain. This study still continues, with current emphasis on the use of an ultrasonic receiver for the identification of flying bats. Other hobbies include photography, hi-fi equipment and tape recording.

David Lack, F.R.S., was born in London in 1910. After reading zoology at Cambridge he taught at Dartington School from 1933 to 1938, colour-ringing robins at first to amuse the pupils, and later spending almost all his spare time and holidays watching robins there. His classic book *The Life of the Robin* was first published in 1943, and appeared as a Penguin ten years later. Since 1945 Dr Lack has been Director of the Edward Grey Institute of Field Ornithology at Oxford. Among his more recent books are *The National Regulation of Animal Numbers* and *Population Studies of Birds*.

Patrick Morris was born in 1943, attended state schools, then read for a degree in zoology at University College London. He went on to study hedgehogs for a Ph.D. and is now assistant lecturer in zoology at Royal Holloway College, London. He has travelled widely in Europe and on expeditions to Asia and Africa. His principal interests are natural history, especially mammals, and photography.

Claude Rivers was born in Kent and educated at Dartford Grammar School. His interest in the life histories of insects dates from his schooldays, and after his marriage he and his wife became well known for their success in breeding tropical silkmoths. In 1953 he went to Cambridge as assistant to Kenneth Smith, F.R.S., to breed and collect insects for research on virus diseases. He is now at the Insect Pathology Unit in the Commonwealth Forestry Institute, Oxford, studying the effect of diseases on insect populations.

K. E. L. Simmons is an ornithologist of wide interests who published his first note in 1947 at the age of 17. Since then he has written over 100 contributions for scientific journals and books on topics such as anting, feathercare, the use of behaviour characters in bird taxonomy, interspecific territorialism, distraction-display and raptor migration. His life-history studies include the graceful warbler (in Egypt), the little ringed plover, the brown booby (on Ascension Island) and his favourite bird – the great crested grebe – on which he is at present working full-time under a grant from the Natural Environment Research Council.

Michael J. A. Simpson was born in Kenya in 1942. He read zoology at Cambridge and earned a Ph.D. in 1967 with his thesis on *The Threat Display of the Siamese Fighting Fish*. Since then he has worked in the psychiatric department of The London Hospital on methods of behavioural description and is currently back in East Africa researching into the social behaviour of wild chimpanzees.

Bernard Stonehouse is a Reader in Zoology at Canterbury University, Christchurch, New Zealand, currently holding a Canadian Commonwealth Research Fellowship at the University of British Columbia, Canada. He has spent four winters and a dozen summers in Antarctica, working mainly with penguins and seals, and was the first biologist to spend a winter studying emperor penguins in their winter quarters. He published his book, *Penguins*, in 1968, and is at present working on their thermoregulation and general biology.

Lancelot Tickell gained a B.Sc. (Wales) in 1954 and from that year until 1957 was employed at the Signey Island (South Orkneys) base of the British Antarctic Survey, as meteorologist, mountaineer, biologist and base-leader. After a year writing up his researches at the Edward Grey Institute in Oxford he organised his own South Georgia Biological Expedition and started work on the wandering albatross. Three more expeditions to South Georgia financed by the United States National Science Foundation, enabled him to prepare a D.Sc. thesis, accepted in 1966. From then till 1968 he was warden naturalist in Shetland for the Nature Conservancy and is currently lecturing at Makerere College, Uganda.

Stephanie Tyler (née Monk) was born in North Yorkshire in 1944 but soon moved to Lincolnshire where she developed a keen interest in all branches of Natural History. Educated at Christ's Hospital Girls' High School, Lincoln, and Girton College, Cambridge, where she read natural sciences and then zoology, she worked for three years on the behaviour of ponies in the New Forest for a Ph.D. She married in 1966 and is now living in Wiltshire where her husband is a veterinary surgeon.